BASS
on the
FLY

A. D. LIVINGSTON

RAGGED MOUNTAIN PRESS
CAMDEN, MAINE

For Dr. Helen N. Livingston,
who seems to have forgiven me
for losing her 8-pound largemouth
at the net some years ago.

Published by Ragged Mountain Press

10 9 8 7 6 5 4 3 2 1

Copyright © 1994 Ragged Mountain Press, an imprint of TAB Books. TAB Books is a division of McGraw-Hill, Inc.

Library of Congress Cataloging in Publication Data
Livingston, A. D., 1932–
　　　Bass on the fly /A. D. Livingston.--2nd ed.
　　　　　p.　　cm.
　　　Rev. ed. of: Fly-rodding for bass. 1 st ed. 1976.
　　　Includes index.
　　　ISBN 0-07-038151-8 (alk. paper)
　　　1.Black bass fishing. 2. Fly fishing. I. Livingston, A. D., 1932– Fly rodding for bass. II. Title.
SH1.L55 1994
799.1'758--dc20.　　　　　　　　　　　93-47194
　　　　　　　　　　　　　　　　　　　　CIP

Questions regarding the content of this book should be addressed to:

Ragged Mountain Press
P.O. Box 220
Camden, ME 04843

Questions regarding the ordering of this book should be addressed to:

TAB Books
A Division of McGraw-Hill, Inc.
Blue Ridge Summit, PA 17294
1-800-233-1128

A portion of the profits from the sale of each Ragged Mountain Press book is donated to an environmental cause.

♳ *Bass on the Fly* is printed on 60-pound Renew Opaque Vellum, an acid-free paper that contains 50 percent recycled waste paper (preconsumer) and 10 percent postconsumer waste paper.

Printed by R. R. Donnelley, Harrisonburg, Virginia.
Design by Carol Gillette
Part, chapter opening, and text illustrations on pages 49 (top), 52, 53, 56, 57, 59, 60, 67, 72, 73 (bottom), 74, 117, 125 by Chris Armstrong.
Production by Molly Mulhern
Edited by Jim Babb, Anne Greenleaf, and Pamela Benner

C O N T E N T S

Other Books by A. D. Livingston

Luremaking: The Art and Science of Spinnerbaits, Buzzbaits, Jigs, and Other Leadheads

Venison Cookbook

Edible Plants and Animals: Unusual Foods from Aardvarks to Zamia (with Dr. Helen N. Livingston)

Grilling, Smoking, and Barbecuing

Cast Iron Cooking

Good Vittles: One Man's Meat, a Few Vegetables, and a Drink or Two

Outdoor Life's Complete Fish & Game Cookbook

Fishing for Bass

Advanced Bass Tackle and Boats

Fly-rodding for Bass (extensively revised as *Bass on the Fly*)

Tying Bass Bugs and Flies

Poker Strategy and Winning Play

The Sky's the Limit (a novel)

Though I have written mostly about trout for the past 25 years, I have a deep, defined, and long-standing affection for bass. Except for a freak catch or two of trout, bass were the first "game" fish I pursued. I fished for largemouth in a Berkshire-foothills lake—with nightcrawlers, frogs, newts, crayfish, sunnies, Flatfish, and Jitterbugs—and then for smallmouth in a nearby river, with spinners. And I fished a lot for smallmouth in the St. Lawrence River, with live shiners fished deep.

When I fell in love with the special pleasures of fly fishing, I tried for bass again, first with popping bugs, which are still my first choice. I have never felt an interest in returning to bait or lures. The fly rod, as A. D. Livingston wisely says, "will at times catch more bass." It will. And that is one of the chief reasons for using it while the bassin' world has exploded with thousands of new lures, rods, reels, boats, and more gadgets and tools than one would have believed could be used in a lifetime.

But there are other reasons as well, and A. D. suggests them throughout his helpful primer on fly-rodding for bass. The basic rhythm of fly fishing, with its rhythmic casting of line (rather than weighted lure) and its increasing versatility *involves* the fisherman in a compelling way. The flip of the wrist that is the basis of spinning or baitcasting is replaced by the rhythmic back-and-forth movement of rod arm and line hand, in unison, so that the fly line unfolds gracefully in the backcast and then is punched forward. The working of the fly line in the air takes a bit more learning than other forms of fishing, but the basic technique can be learned in a few days. And fly fishing is certainly a more methodical technique; you don't cast as much, you cover less water more carefully, and you participate more in each cast, retrieve, and the playing of the fish on a long rod with a single-action reel. And, as A. D. proposes, there are times when flies will simply take more fish.

One reason for this is the lightness and flexibility of a fly made of fur and feathers, which responds in a lifelike manner to the slightest manipulation. Retrieve even the best sinking lure too slowly and it will sink to the bottom, while a fly can be teased, twitched, drawn to dip and dart, brought to a cold stop, and started again in a varying series of zigzag strips. And nothing in my fishing experience has ever matched for excitement the explosion a largemouth makes when it crashes up for a twitched deer-hair bug or foam popper near the lily pads at dusk.

A. D. is alert to the revolution in bass tackle, techniques, and knowledge. With his shrewd, practical, no-nonsense mind he chooses the best from long-proven tools and techniques and adds the best of the new. Always—with his frank and engaging wit—he cuts through the layers of bilge that have accumulated around the sport.

"Anyone guilty of habitual jiggerpoling with a fine fly rod," he says, after introducing a maverick technique, "ought to have his name struck from the Orvis mailing list."

And, getting to the heart of things: "The secret of successful bass fishing boils down to locating the fish and then knowing how to catch them."

That's about as trim and compact and true a maxim as you'd want. And A. D. shares his deft knowledge of both the finding and the catching in this sensible book. He will help any trout fisherman make a quick and happy transition to bass and also help all good spin- and baitcasting bass fishermen learn the pleasures and great practicality of fly fishing for this great gamefish.

Nick Lyons

P R E F A C E When I first wrote this preface, I rambled on for five or six pages, exploring in my mind the virtues of fishing for bass with a fly rod. Then I decided to come right to the point: The best reason for using a fly rod is that it will at times catch more bass. That's right. At times bugs and flies will outfish hardware, live bait, and even soft plastic worms. I have proved this, at least to my own satisfaction, on a number of occasions. Why? I believe it's how the lure is presented. Anything cast with spinning gear, or even baitcasting gear, is likely to splash down in the water. A bug or a fly, though, can be made to roll over and settle down gently—a delivery difficult to match with any other casting gear, and it can be deadly on skittish bass in shallow water.

In any case, more and more anglers are going after black bass with fly rods. Some are experienced bass specialists who have added a fly rod to their several baitcasting and spinning rigs. Others are trout anglers who, finding wild trout fast disappearing from the streams in some areas, decide to go after bass. I hope that the bass specialists will be pleased, if somewhat surprised, to learn that a fly rod is a real aid to catching fish, not merely something light and sporting. And I trust that the trout angler disillusioned with put-and-take hatchery fish will find the black bass— one of the most intelligent of freshwater gamefish and certainly one of the world's great predators—to be a worthy opponent, one that is now plentiful, North, South, East, and West. In fact, the bass's habitat continues to increase with every new dam being built here and abroad for hydroelectric power, flood control, and navigational purposes, with every state or city lake built for recreation and water supply, and with every new farm pond from coast to coast. I'd guess that the bass's habitat, despite a few setbacks here and there, has doubled within the last 40 years. Even such dusty states as Oklahoma now have excellent bass fishing, and lots of it.

I'm not going to call all trout anglers cheapskates, but since in all probability I've already riled them up I might as well give another good reason for fishing for bass with a fly rod: It is by far the cheapest way to fish these days. A fly rod can be expensive, but it doesn't have to be, and an adequate reel for bass fishing can cost under $10. Flies or bugs are inexpensive (except for some of the newer saltwater creations such as McCrabs, which can be deadly on brackish water bass), typically selling for half the price of the popular balsa-wood Rapalas. At upwards of $40, fly line may seem expensive, but a good level line can be had for under $10, and is all you *really* need for bass fishing. Moreover, a good fly line can last decades with reasonable care, whereas the bass angler using either spinning gear or baitcasting gear spooled with monofilament will have to change lines on almost every outing. Further, anyone who has priced a dozen shiners or a box of crickets lately will have to concede that fly-rodding is cheaper than fishing with live bait—and, in the hands of an expert, is usually more productive.

I rest my case, at least for the time being. Keep your bug sharp and your backcast high.

I started working on the first edition of this book almost a quarter of a century ago, when my wife and I were living on Timucuan Island in Florida's Lake Weir, 50 or 60 miles north of the present Disney World. This beautiful clear-water lake is on the edge of Florida's Big Scrub, where Marjorie Kinnen Rawlings set *The Yearling*. In the small town of Oklawaha, across the main lake from our island, Ma Barker and her boys holed up in a two-story wooden house and shot it out with the FBI in the early 1930s. Nothing else happened there for a long time.

During the late 1940s, I spent some time fishing Lake Weir from a weekly rental cabin in Oklawaha. Mostly, we caught shellcrackers (redear sunfish). Of course we didn't have a clue where to fish on such a large lake, but a local fellow, either a guide or a friend or both, helped us out by diving off the boat and swimming about under the water until he located bedding fish. He had no fins or scuba gear, and I was amazed, and sometimes a little frightened, at how long he could go before surfacing for air. Sometimes I would have to breathe two or three times while waiting and watching. But he found the fish. Big ones, as I remember them.

My brother-in-law from Jacksonville had brought along a brand new Shakespeare Wonderod with him. It was the first fiberglass fly rod I had ever seen, and both of us were eager to try it out as soon as we had taught the womenfolk and children how to catch shellcrackers. But Weir was a rather large lake and the wind was something of a problem. Paddling, I couldn't hold the 14-foot cypress rental boat in casting position for him and, to be honest, he hadn't yet mastered the fly rod. We finally gave it up and trolled a little, catching a huge chain pickerel on a deep-diving River Runt plug.

Later, he caught some big bluegills and a few small bass on a cork bug by wading in the grass along the edges of the lake. The banks of the lake were impassable, being grown up with wax myrtle trees and thick bushes. He wanted a large bass, and we ended up anchoring the boat and fishing with large shiners, which, of course, were caught by a professional shiner man on the lake. (This was not an unusual profession in Florida back then. These days, most of the shiners sold at the "Beer, Bait, and Baloney" stops near good fishing holes are hatchery raised and aren't as good as wild shiners for very large bass.) But this is slow fishing; you can go for hours and days without a bite, hardly the sort of thing to occupy a strapping boy and a sport with a new Wonderod.

There were lots of bass in Weir, but it was difficult to fish for them by today's standards. Years later—during the early 1970s—my wife and I were lucky enough to purchase a cozy little house with a red tile roof on a white beach on Lake Weir's Timucuan Island, across the blue waters from Oklawaha. Although our cove wasn't as windy as the main lake, I bought an electric trolling motor (which is seldom used for trolling) and mounted it on the bow of a 12-foot jonboat. This rig greatly increased my ability to catch bluegills and bass with a fly rod simply because it made boat handling easier, permitting me to hold the boat in casting position along a weed line with a foot-controlled pedal while leaving both hands free for working the fly rod and landing fish. Catching 40 or 50 bluegills and a limit of bass wasn't unusual. When I bought a depthfinder and mounted it on the bow of the boat, I learned more about Lake Weir in a day or two than I had in the previous months. This didn't help me much with the bluegills, but I started catching more and larger bass. The trick was to find suitable cover near deep water.

Then I purchased a 14-foot aluminum bassboat with comfortable swivel seats, and, of course, rigged it with a foot-controlled bow-mounted electric motor and a depthfinder on each end. Thus, from the time of Ma Barker until the early 1970s, anglers saw the introduction of monofilament line and fiberglass rods. Then, suddenly, came the modern bassboat, which depends on comfortable swivel fishing seats, depthfinder, and bow-mounted electric motor. While we lived on the island, we also saw the first graphite fishing rods and high-floating, foam-filled fly lines. Nothing much has happened to bass fishing tackle since then, except that the equipment has been refined. Although bass fishing itself has grown by leaps and bounds, the essential hardware was in place in the 1970s, as were some hot new fishing impoundments, such as Toledo Bend on the Louisiana–Texas border.

Bass fishing started to grow. The boats got faster. Also, things were beginning to stir in rural Central Florida. The little country high school on the hill overlooking Lake Weir doubled its enrollment in two years. People of all sorts moved in from the north and they moved in from the south, getting out of Miami and Tampa. We had the feeling that the population boom had barely started, and a worried old Florida Cracker told me that if I would climb atop the water tank in Weirsdale on a clear day I could see Disney World coming up the road.

That was in the 1970s and I don't want to look at what has happened to Central Florida since then. I feel the same way about bass fishing whenever my editor, Jim Babb, tells me that this book still has the 1970s written all over it. Well, I say, what's wrong with that? The 1970s was the decade of the bassboat and graphite rods. What else has happened to bass fishing? Owing to an entrepreneur named Ray Scott, tournament fishing has grown dramatically. Some of the heroes of the tournament trail started fishing lure companies, TV shows, or both. Their pictures appeared in magazine articles and in advertisements for the latest products. The tournament purses became fatter. Before long, the winner of a major bass tournament could win $100,000 or better, and stood to gain ten times as much in spin-off benefits and endorsements. It was showtime.

We all know what has happened to bass fishing with hardware and soft plastic worms since the early 1970s. But what has happened especially to taking bass on the fly since the introduction of graphite rods and foam-filled fly lines? Not much. The attempts to hold fly-fishing tournaments didn't work too well and never developed into big money competition. In the first fly-rodding bass tournament that I heard about, some of the contestants ended up slinging spinnerbaits instead of casting flies. It's true that we have seen the development of some better subsurface lures and bottom scooters. These are said to imitate waterdogs and such, but the plain truth is that they were inspired by the great success of the plastic worm and are probably no better at taking fish. In short, I don't see that much has happened to require drastic changes in this book—and I told my editor just that.

"Then what's our justification for publishing a new edition, A. D.?" he asked.

"Hold on," I quickly said. "All bass anglers are lure freaks, and the new upside-down lead eye trick alone will be enough to justify this inexpensive little *paperback* edition."

He didn't answer, obviously catching my emphasis on the word "paperback" and not wanting to argue that one again.

"I mentioned Most Whit bugs and Zonkers and Dalhopper Dippers . . . . "

"Divers," he said. "Dahlberg Divers."

"Besides that," I went on, "I've got all sorts of updated material in this book about how to catch bass when they aren't biting."

"Maybe we can do a deluxe hardcover edition later," he said.

*F*ly *fishing* is neither difficult to learn nor strenuous to perform if you have the right gear. But casting a large, heavy, wind-resistant bug with a rod and line designed for tiny dry flies or nymphs is well nigh impossible. Neither impeccable casting form nor sheer muscle power will get a 2/0 bug out 50 feet with the wrong rod, line, and leader. The first step toward easy bass bugging is to balance your tackle, and I hope that the following chapters will be helpful for anyone starting from scratch.

PART 1
SELECTING TACKLE AND GEAR

Anglers who already know the motions and rhythms of fly casting may be in for a cultural shock when switching from a dainty size-16 dry fly to a 2/0 cork bug with a long feather tail. Even equipped with an adequate line and rod they may still have problems. I suggest that they first take a look at their leader (see page 24), making sure that it's stiff enough to turn the bug over. I also suggest that they watch their backcast and adjust their casting rhythm. Large, fluffy bugs slow everything down.

CHAPTER 1

RODS

Once I knew an ex-prize fighter who lived on a 50-acre private lake surrounded by a family-owned citrus grove in Central Florida. One night years ago he was lazing before his TV set while waiting to see a boxing match. Suddenly, a commercial started advertising a new imitation fruit drink called Tang. Upon hearing that the newfangled stuff contained more vitamin C than orange juice, he jumped up and danced around, ready to punch something. "It's a damned lie!" he said. "I've been drinking orange juice all my life." Well, the fact that he had been drinking orange juice all his life had no bearing whatsoever on the vitamin C content of Tang.

I suspect that many anglers apply the same sort of logic, or lack of it, to their fishing rods and to other bass fishing aids, such as new electronic depthfinders. Because an old favorite fits the hand comfortably and has turned many a fish doesn't necessarily make it superior to a newer rod.

Other anglers are outright suckers for anything new. If one of these tackle freaks had been watching the TV commercial, he would have jumped up and sped off to the nearest grocery store in search of the new instant nectar, even if he had seven gallons of fresh orange juice in the refrigerator. If the store happened to be closed, he would roust the manager in the middle of the night. If he couldn't find any of the new stuff in local stores, he would telephone the manufacturer long distance to place a rush order for two dozen cases, C.O.D. He would then lie awake at night waiting for the stuff to arrive, his mouth juicy, his taste buds tangy, his vim rising just at the thought of that vitamin C.

Nothing I say here is likely to change anglers of either extreme. But I do believe that the angler who has been using the same old rod for 30 years will improve his casting and enjoy it more if he tries a carefully selected modern stick. I also believe that an angler who thinks that a new space-age wand will land a record bass for him will probably catch more fish by getting out on the lake instead of swishing rods around in tackle shops.

I first broke the Tang story back in 1976—when the first edition of this book came out. Of course, back then I was talking about making the switch from fiberglass to the new graphite rods while, at the same time, taking a pot shot at the sticklers who still wielded bamboo fly rods. At that time, graphite fiber material was quite expensive and the manufacturing technology was new. Today, the switch to graphite rods is not quite so drastic if you happen to own an old fiberglass rod.

In any case, fly rods have been greatly improved in recent years, and the modern angler has a very wide range of quality rods from which to choose. For the sake of discussion, I'll cover modern rod materials by topic, but in practice it's sometimes hard to tell what's what, even if you read the advertisements and the labels on the rod blank.

FIBERGLASS

From a casting standpoint, fiberglass may not be the ideal stuff from which to manufacture rod blanks, but it does make a very good fishing stick. It's tough. It's light compared with the old steel or bamboo rods. It doesn't rot and, in general, it can be kicked around more than bamboo or graphite. There is no shortage of the material, and it lends itself well to mass production. What's more, modern manufacturing processes have vastly improved fiberglass rods since they were introduced shortly after World War II. Until recently, fiberglass rods dominated the market, and this itself was an advantage simply because a wide choice of dependable blanks became available at reasonable prices. It was a good rod for the masses— much better than steel rods, much better than cheap bamboo rods, and much less expensive than quality bamboo rods.

The difference between an expensive fiberglass rod and an inexpensive one is more than just the quality of the blank; it's the fittings and workmanship required to finish off the rod. Indeed, both an expensive and an inexpensive rod might have been made from identical off-the-shelf blanks.

Although a glance through the mail-order catalogs and a slow walk down the rod racks of the better tackle shops might indicate that fiberglass is no longer a player in fishing rods, this is simply not the case. It's just that nobody advertises fiberglass any more. Thus, a cheap graphite rod might be billed as having "graphite power." Further, all of the composites are going to be called "graphite composites," not "fiberglass composites." If truth in advertising is ever enforced in the tackle industry, we might well see a renaissance of the fiberglass fly rod.

GRAPHITE

I might have been the first serious bass fisherman to write about graphite rods. At the time, back in the 1960s, I was writing a column on the benefits of space research for *Space Information Digest*, a NASA publication. While trying to sell the American people on the space program, NASA had started looking for ways to use new materials and technology in the real world. High-modulus graphite was one of these, and was believed to have potential in fishing rods and other products. Of course, I included the fishing rods in my NASA column on high-modulus graphite and in a more general article called "Satellites for Sportsmen" that I did for *Field & Stream*.

I was therefore pleased, years later, to see graphite rods actually appearing on the market. (I might add that I didn't pick up on aluminum oxide for fishing rod guides, and I pooped up some stuff, such as beryllium beams, that never amounted to a damn in fishing tackle.) In any case, high-modulus graphite is tough, stiff, and light. A rod blank made of graphite fibers is about 25-percent lighter than a comparable fiberglass blank. But these figures are only for the blanks; the handles and fittings weigh about the same, and the weights of finished rods might differ by not much more than an ounce. On the other hand, I for one appreciate even an ounce of savings in weight, especially when I'm making repeated casts with a heavy fly line and bass bugs.

Another point is that a typical graphite rod is much smaller in diameter than a typical fiberglass rod; this reduces wind resistance, which might be more important than a savings in weight over a long day of casting.

When they were first introduced for fishing more than 20 years ago, graphite rods were a little too expensive for most of us, although I bought one in the name of research. The really top-line graphites are still expensive ($275 to $450), but a number of good sticks are available for under $150. The more expensive rods are predominantly graphite as billed, although some of them might contain other material to slightly alter the characteristics of a 100-percent graphite blank. In short, graphite is quite stiff and a little too brittle. Although it casts well and is strong under a bending load, a sharp nick on the blank might well cause it to break. In fact, a good many expensive graphite rods have been broken while bouncing around on the deck of a bassboat. But the modern rods are better in this regard than the original graphite rods, and no doubt improvements will continue.

COMPOSITES

Graphite is definitely the "in" stuff for modern rods, but the material is still expensive compared with fiberglass. For this reason, fiberglass is often used in graphite "composites" to reduce the price and, sometimes, to alter the properties of the rod. There are far too many designs on the market these days to make generalizations, but often a "composite rod" has lots of graphite in the butt end to reduce the weight and lots of fiberglass in the tip end to enhance the bending properties. If carried too far, however, such a rod will seem tip-heavy to accomplished rod shakers.

The composites have all but replaced pure fiberglass rods, and, in most cases, they are better than pure fiberglass. The beginner, who may not want to plunk down the money for a predominantly graphite stick, will probably end up with a composite. The exact proportion of fiberglass to graphite in such a rod is difficult to determine, but as a rule a rod high in graphite will have a small butt section. This rule may change at any time, however, and remember that a solid fiberglass rod can also have a small butt section. Moreover, I must emphasize that merely knowing the graphite content of a rod guarantees nothing. I have seen some very good rods made from pure fiberglass.

BAMBOO

A top-quality bamboo rod is a thing of beauty and has some highly desirable casting qualities. Bamboo is a little stiffer than fiberglass, but it casts nicely. Fans claim that a bamboo rod "seems to cast itself." Bamboo is heavier than either fiberglass or graphite, making it better for stalking trout with lightweight lines and tiny flies than for making repeated casts for bass with large bugs.

A big disadvantage is that top-quality raw materials are in short supply and that building a split-bamboo rod requires a lot of craftsmanship, which means that top-notch bamboo rods are expensive—from $800 to more than $2,000.

In short, my objection to bamboo is based not on casting performance but on price and practical fishing considerations. Personally, I would be uncomfortable fishing with anything that costs $2,000. I would like to have one, though, to look at like a work of art.

BORON

A lot of people went for boron rods a few years back and were impressed with the rod's sensitivity. I used one for a while, but the material has pretty much dropped out of the rod market, at least for the time being, because it breaks so easily. New developments and new bonding agents, however, may make boron or other new fibers more feasible in rods of the future. But I was in the fishing tackle business long enough to know that it's best to give anything new a few years, unless of course you're suffering from scurvy and need some vitamin C fast.

A part from material, a rod blank's performance depends largely on action, weight, and length.

ACTION

Rod blanks are classified as slow, medium, fast, and extra-fast depending on how they bend under a load. It's all a matter of time and timing. A rod blank that bends from tip to butt during casting, and that takes longer to straighten after bending, is a slow rod. If it bends only in the tip end and recovers quickly, it's a fast rod. Medium, obviously, is somewhere in between.

I prefer a slow rod for bass fishing because it works better for me, and because it isn't as tiring to cast as a fast rod. A slow, full-flex rod can become almost an extension of the casting arm, permitting a smooth, continuous power stroke. But casting isn't the only consideration. A fast rod with a stiff midsection and butt is better for setting large hooks and is also better for horsing bass out of treetops. A good compromise is a medium-action rod, whether it be for baitcasting, spinning, or fly fishing.

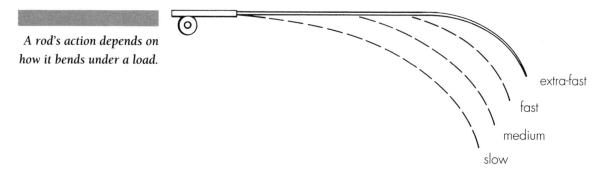

A rod's action depends on how it bends under a load.

Unfortunately, it's difficult to tell from some manufacturers' literature, or from the description in some mail-order catalogs, exactly which action a rod has. Some outfits don't even mention rod action, as if the fact that they market the stick is all one needs to know. Others specify "bass action," "steelhead action," and so on. Still others use such terms as "power" and "taper." Most manufacturers of quality rods, however, and most mail-order houses, will happily answer your questions about rod actions. In a tackle shop, you may or may not get a good answer. (I've seen some tackle shops that put open-faced spinning reels on saltwater popping rods!) The best bet, when considering a rod off the rack, is to test the action yourself. Most anglers take a rod off a rack and swish it up and down, but the correct way to study the action is to jam the butt against your belly, hold the handle with both hands, and swish the rod horizontally. Watch how and where it bends and you can pretty much determine its action. This method is generally foolproof in detecting fast, tip-action sticks, although sometimes the distinction between slow and medium is hard to discern. Some fly-fishing specialty shops equipped with casting ranges or pools will let you *try* a number of rods before finally settling on the one you feel most comfortable using. In the end, this may be the best way to buy a rod, although these shops carry mostly high-end merchandise.

WEIGHT

The weight or "power" of a rod is a separate design variable, not to be confused with action, or even with the rod's physical weight. The weight of any good rod is matched to the weight it was designed to cast, regardless of whether that weight be plug, live bait, or fly line. You simply can't cast a heavy weight satisfactorily with a light rod, or a light weight with a heavy rod.

Fortunately, fly-rod manufacturers now rate their blanks in accordance with the line-weight standards established by AFTMA (American Fishing Tackle Manufacturers' Association). Most of the better rods are marked clearly with the size or weight of the line they are designed to cast. All the better mail-order houses list this information in their catalog specifications of rods and rod blanks.

Although beginners will do well to match rod and line strictly according to the manufacturer's recommendations, there is some room for deviation. Most rods perform pretty well with a line one size larger or one size smaller than the rod manufacturer's specification. It's been my experience, however, that rods used for bass fishing work better slightly overloaded than underloaded. For one thing—and this is basic—it takes a heavier line to carry a bass bug. For another, bass anglers frequently make short casts, which are generally a little easier to execute with a slightly overloaded rod. The best bet, however, is to stick with the rod manufacturer's recommendations unless you have good reason to experiment.

To be honest, I prefer a 7-weight graphite rod for casting a medium bug on an 8-weight level line, and an 8-weight rod for casting a 9-weight level line (more on line weights in chapter 3). A smaller rod is also lighter and easier to wield, and, after all, it's difficult to overload a rod on a short cast. In other words, the load depends in large measure on how much line is being cast. If I were going on the salt flats, where distance casting is more important than on the typical bass pond, I might even prefer to go a step or two in the other direction.

I might add that manufacturers may make mistakes from time to time when classifying certain rods. I've seen a 9-weight fiberglass rod that was far too heavy for practical bass fishing. (It might have been more suited to an 11-weight line.) I should point out that the whole fishing tackle industry does some screwy things, based on what sells.

LENGTH

Within reason, the longer the rod the greater the distance it will cast a fly line. There are limits, however, beyond which a rod simply becomes unwieldy. For general bass fishing, an 8½-foot fiberglass rod of suitable weight and action is about right. An 8-foot rod will do, and so will a 9-footer. But I feel that 9-foot fiberglass rods designed for saltwater use or for distance casting will quickly wear out a bass angler; although these long, hefty rods might cast bass bugs wondrously for a while, they are simply too heavy to wield all day, cast after cast.

On the other hand, a 9- or 9½-foot graphite rod of the right line weight works fine for most bass bugging. If you are bass fishing from a boat, a longer graphite rod makes the pickup easier, which is important when trying to lift some bass bugs off the water. A disadvantage is that such a long rod can make short, accurate casts more difficult, and, if my experience is typical, most bass anglers make a lot of casts under 30 feet.

On the short side, I wouldn't recommend any stick less than 8 feet long—and limited distance isn't the only reason. It's a matter of timing. Short rods stiff enough to handle a bass bug line require a much faster tempo, making timing critical. What's more, short, stiff rods are downright dangerous when casting heavy bugs. I tried to fish with a stiff 7-foot rod designed to take an 8-weight line, but I soon put the thing down because I didn't want a bass bug in my ear. And short rods make picking up heavy bugs and line difficult, which gets the backcast off to a bad start, which in turn makes the forward cast difficult.

I f I had to recommend an all-purpose bass rod, I would come up with an 8½-foot 8-weight medium- or slow-action fiberglass or composite fly rod, or a 9 ½-foot 8-weight medium- or slow-action graphite rod. Neither rod would be ideal for every aspect of bass fishing, but either would do just about anything, anytime, anywhere, either for smallmouth or largemouth. Indeed, it might even be better to stick with such a basic rod and learn how to use it well instead of jumping from one length and action to another.

In any case, here are a few additional points to consider when selecting and using a fly rod.

GUIDES AND TIPS

In normal fly fishing, the rod guides and tip aren't subjected to as much wear and friction as they are in baitcasting and spinning with artificial lures, since the entire length of the fly line isn't shot through and pulled back over the guides on every cast. After working out some line, a fly fisherman might make any number of casts without stripping in or shooting out more than a few feet of line. Also, fly-rod lures are generally fished slower than hardware and aren't usually retrieved all the way to the rod tip. Even so, a fly rod's guides and tip should be inspected from time to time. A good fly line is expensive, and there's no point in wearing it out with abrasive guides and tip.

Traditionally, fly rods are fitted with snake guides, except for a stripping guide or two on the butt end. Snake guides are made from hard-chromed wire in the shape of an open spiral, with the ends flattened to enable the rod winding thread to bind them tightly to the blank. The tip is usually made from a pear-shaped loop of wire with the ends soldered into a metal tube, which in turn fits over the end of the rod blank. A big advantage of wire guides and tips is their light weight.

Stripping guides consist of a metal frame fitted with a hard ring, much like the guides on better baitcasting rods. I personally prefer aluminum-oxide or "ceramic" rings to metal ones, but tungsten carbide or hard stainless steel rings are sometimes used.

Some fly rods designed for distance shooting have been fitted with single-footed aluminum-oxide guides. These guides reduce friction, thereby permitting longer casts. They also help keep the line away from the blank, which reduces rod slap. If you do a lot of distance casting, then you certainly should consider replacing standard wire snake guides with lightweight ring guides. But remember that you can alter the action of a rod by tampering even slightly with the weight or the spacing of the guides. For ordinary bass fishing, I recommend standard snake guides with one or two aluminum-oxide stripping guides on the butt end.

GRIPS

Most fly-rod grips are made by slipping cork rings over the rod blank, setting them with glue, and then shaping them. Half a dozen shapes have become more or less standard, but cigar-shaped grips are probably more common than all the rest put together. Any grip that is comfortable throughout the cast is satisfactory, although I should note that some very light fly rods are fitted with grips that are just too small, at least for me. They may be all right for a few casts, but not for a hard day's bass fishing.

Most of the better off-the-shelf fly rods are available only in a standard grip. If you're fussy about grips and want something especially for your hand, the best bet is to talk to a rodmaker. Or do it yourself. Many tackle shops and mail-order houses market cork rings, reel seats, and other rodmaking tools and materials.

Penn's IMS-6890 fly-rod handle has a full-wells cork grip, uplocking reel seat, and an extension butt. (Courtesy Penn Fishing Tackle)

REEL SEATS

Most of the inexpensive or moderately priced fly rods are fitted with fixed reel seats made from anodized aluminum alloy. Usually, a hood (or cup) fixed to the end of the rod receives one end of the reel's foot. A similar hood slides up and down a barrel (which is threaded on one end) and can be tightened onto the forward reel foot by knurled rings. Double-locking seats have two knurled rings, and are more secure. Some of the more expensive rods have a hardwood barrel with nickel-silver screw mechanisms on the forward end. Some have uplocking reel seats; some have downlocking. Frankly, I don't see any mechanical advantage of one type over the other.

Very light rods, and a few heavier sticks, often have the entire reel seat made of cork, and the reel is held in place by two metal friction rings, without any sort of screw mechanism. I own a 1¾-ounce rod fitted with sliding rings, and they work very well. Frankly, I would just as soon have simple rings on all my fly rods (and on light spinning rods).

EXTENSION BUTTS

Some of the more expensive rods come with extension butts attached to the end of the reel seat. About 1½ to 2 inches long, these butts (some of which are detachable) are designed to fit comfortably against one's belly when battling a large fish. They might come in handy for fighting a tarpon or even a streaking bonefish, but they aren't necessary for brawling with bass.

FERRULES

In order to avoid such marketing terms as "ferruleless ferrules," I'll hereby define a fishing-rod ferrule as any plug-and-socket arrangement that joins together two sections of a rod. I prefer one-piece blanks for baitcasting and for most spinning rods, but fly rods almost have to break apart for the convenience of toting them around. The fewer the ferrules, however, the more continuous and uniform the blank. In short, I prefer two-piece fly rods to three-piece rods.

Most of the better fiberglass rods made these days have glass-to-glass ferrules; graphite rods have graphite-to-graphite ferrules. Bamboo rods usually have nickel-silver ferrules, and some custom-made glass or graphite rods are fitted with anodized aluminum ferrules with replaceable rubber O-rings on the plug. Arguments can be made for and against any of the better-quality ferrules. Glass-to-glass or graphite-to-graphite ferrules are generally trouble free and don't stick together as often as metal ferrules; if they're damaged, however, or if they wear too much, the rod owner has serious problems. Metal ferrules can be replaced easily, but they're prone to bind and can be a pain in the neck. Proper care and attention to ferrules can save you time in the long run. Ferrules should always be unplugged when the fishing trip is over.

From a casting viewpoint, I prefer glass-to-glass or graphite-to-graphite ferrules simply because they bend with the rod more than metal ferrules do. They have, in fact, become pretty much standard on the better rods, except for split-bamboo sticks.

I hate to hem and haw too much before getting to the bottom line, but the plain truth is that making fishing rods isn't yet an exact science. Off-the-shelf rods billed as identical are sometimes quite different, and of course custom-made rods vary widely. One of my favorite fiberglass rods happens to be an 8-foot River Rat, which I bought through mail order some years ago. I liked it so much that I immediately ordered another one, but the second one wasn't the same rod. I don't know why.

CHAPTER 2

Fly Reels

It's been said that a fly reel's sole function is to store line. I've said it myself. A fly reel does retrieve slack line and can sometimes help battle a large fish, but since the spool doesn't actually pay out line during the cast, the importance of good reel design has been belittled. But how a fly reel stores line can either facilitate or foil easy casting, especially when you're going for distance. Line coiled tightly on a small-diameter spool, for instance, can result in a tangled corkscrew of a cast.

There are three basic types of fly reels: single-action, multiplier, and automatic. The ideal fly reel of any type is narrow (about 1 inch) with a large-diameter spool (from 3 to 4 inches, depending on the size of the fly line and the amount of backing line used). Such a spool has two definite advantages. First, the large diameter minimizes "coil set" in the fly line. Coiled and kinky line makes shooting difficult, and in extreme cases can tangle a line so badly that it knots, usually jamming at a rod guide when you have a large fish on. Second, a large, full spool makes for a fast retrieve, which helps retrieve slack line quickly—important when working some bass bugs or when a hooked fish runs toward you. In addition, the large-diameter spool can be ventilated with holes in the sides, and the narrow span permits air to circulate through the wet, spooled line.

Here are some additional considerations to keep in mind when choosing a fly reel:

- A good drag system is highly desirable on any reel, especially on a fly reel used with a light leader tippet.

- Because a fly line is only 30 or 35 yards long, the reel should have sufficient capacity for backing line. Many anglers err by thinking only of weight, and get a reel that's too small. I've made that mistake myself. Once I ordered an automatic reel that wouldn't even hold all the size-9 fly line I intended to use, much less 100 yards of backing.

- A reel with interchangeable spools means you'll be able to switch quickly from one fly line to another; usually from a floating to a sinking line. Some anglers use three or even four spools.

- A click ratchet or similar mechanism is needed to prevent the spool from turning too fast and fouling the line.

SINGLE-ACTION REELS

If I had to choose one reel for all my fly fishing, I would quickly take a good single-action model with a large-diameter spool. These reels are mechanically simple, light in weight, and generally trouble free. The term "single action" refers to a reel with a 1-to-1 retrieve ratio; a knob mounted near the rim turns the reel spool directly, without a gear train. The only disadvantage of single-action reels is that taking up slack line is slow when compared with multiplying or automatic fly reels. Although a faster retrieve may be desirable at times, a single-action with a large-diameter spool is usually quite adequate for bass fishing and for most other forms of fly fishing. A 4-inch diameter reel, for example, hauls in about a foot of line per revolution when the spool is filled to capacity.

Scientific Anglers System 2-M fly reel (Courtesy Scientific Anglers)

Cheaper single-action reels have no drag system, except possibly for a nonadjustable click ratchet. Better models have either an internal drag that works on some sort of adjustable brake system, a manual "rim" drag, or both. I prefer reels with a rim drag, in which at least part of the outer side of the revolving spool is accessible for "palming." When a fish is taking out line, you cup the rim in your hand and adjust the pressure on the spool. Experienced anglers can instantly increase or decrease the drag.

Most of the better single-action fly reels have interchangeable spools—a highly desirable feature well suited to single-action reels. Some of the more expensive reels have a one-sided solid frame, which permits the interchangeable spools to snap on and off in a second, without pinching the line between frame and rim; such a spool is ideal for rim braking. On some less expensive reels, the spool fits inside a cage-type frame, a design that complicates rim braking. Some of these cage reels, however, do have a good internal, adjustable drag system, as well as interchangeable spools.

MULTIPLYING REELS

A multiplying reel has a true handle, fitted into the center of the spool and attached to a gear train, which usually turns the spool at a ratio of about 3 to 1 or better. The advantage of a multiplying reel is that it takes up slack line faster than a single-action reel, which can be quite helpful, and can even save the day when a fast fish runs toward you.

Multiplying reels are unnecessary for bass fishing, and, frankly, I prefer the simplicity of single-action reels. But any angler who uses his bass rig to go after bigger, faster game should certainly consider a multiplier.

AUTOMATIC REELS

In the late 1800s, Herman W. Martin, founder of the Martin Reel Company, lost a prize fish because his fly line tangled in the bottom of his boat. He subsequently invented a fly reel that automatically picked up excess or slack line. However ingenious for the times, the first automatics were crude-looking contraptions compared with today's streamlined models.

Most automatic fly reels work on a loaded-spring principle. When line is stripped off the reel, the spool revolves and tightens a spring. When the retrieve trigger is depressed with the pinkie of the rod hand, the spring tension is released and the spring turns the spool, zipping in the line. The better automatic reels have a "free-stripping" feature, which allows fly line and backing line to be paid out without overloading the spring. Some automatics also have a spring-tensioning device so that the spring can be loaded without stripping off line, and some models have a release so that the spring won't have to be stored under tension.

The big advantage of automatics is that they can quickly take in excess line and get it out from underfoot. (Standing on a fly line, especially in a boat or on a rocky bank, is a major source of line wear and cracking.) In addition, the rapid retrieve can be very helpful when a fish runs toward you.

There are, however, several disadvantages to automatic fly reels:

• Automatics are generally a good deal heavier than manual fly reels.

• Automatics don't have the line capacity of the larger manual reels of the same weight. This limited line capacity isn't as critical in bass angling as it is in saltwater fishing, but I personally like to have a lot of backing line available just in case I need it. In other words, if I'm going to be using a heavy reel, I prefer to have the weight in backing line instead of in steel springs and related mechanisms.

- Typically, an automatic reel's spool has a smaller diameter than a spool on a manual reel of comparable weight. Consequently, line coil is more of a problem with automatics.

- Because of its mechanical complexity, it's more difficult to design an automatic reel with interchangeable spools. Although some automatics do feature interchangeable spools, the change-out is not as quick as on single-action reels.

- Automatics are more apt to develop mechanical problems.

- Lacking handles or manual cranks, automatic reels can't be used for playing down large fish.

In my opinion, the disadvantages of automatics far outweigh the advantages of fast line pickup. I have, however, caught lots of bass with an automatic reel. They come in handy for night fishing, when tangled lines are more likely to occur, especially if the angler is using a foot-controlled electric motor.

Fly reel prices vary drastically. My first reel, if I remember correctly, cost only $1.98 some years back. It has served me well, and is still usable. I do, however, prefer to have a more sophisticated reel, especially when I'm in lunker-bass country or when bass bugging in waters where larger gamefish may hit. At least that's what I tell myself. Part of the whole truth is that I studied mechanical engineering and like precision gear. Up to a point. Some fly reels cost $750. That's too much for a fly-line cage.

All things considered, I would advise budget-minded anglers to skimp on the reel in order to invest in a good rod.

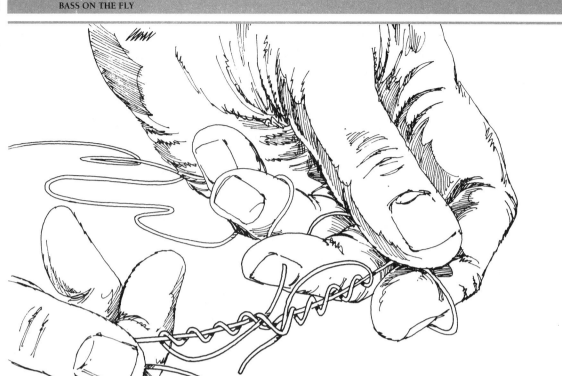

CHAPTER 3

LINES, LEADERS, AND KNOTS

Choice of line is important in all types of fly-rodding, especially when casting, or trying to cast, heavy, wind-resistant bugs. I don't intend to argue here whether the line is more important than the rod, but if you're going to mismatch your gear it's better to err with a heavy line on a light rod than with a light line on a heavy rod.

More than one bass angler accustomed to baitcasting and spinning gear has bought an adequate fly rod but equipped it with a line too light for bass bugging. What they fail to realize is that in fly fishing they're casting a heavy line that pulls a lightweight lure behind it, whereas in baitcasting and spinning they cast a heavy lure that pulls a lightweight line. The heavier the plug, the heavier the line it will pull; the heavier the fly line, the heavier the bug it will pull. In baitcasting or spinning, the rod is matched to the weight of the lure; in fly fishing, the rod is matched to the weight of the line, which in turn is (or should be) selected on the basis of the fly or bug that one intends to cast.

In short, it isn't uncommon for an experienced bass fisherman to purchase the wrong fly line, and to conclude, after a bout or two on the lake, that fly fishing is a difficult thing. Moreover, some bass anglers are likely to be taken aback by the price of a top-notch fly line, which may run close to $50. Why so much for only 30 yards of line when a spinning reel or baitcasting reel can be spooled with 100 yards of line for $5? Because, unlike extruded monofilament and braided lines of uniform diameter and materials, a fly line is a complex composite of an outer coating over a central braided core, and the more expensive lines are tapered very precisely. In addition, floating lines must float and sinking lines must sink at a predetermined rate, which increases the complexity and manufacturing costs. Despite the high initial cost, however, a good fly line is actually cheaper over the long run than either spinning or baitcasting line. With proper care, a good fly line can be used for many years, whereas monofilament and braided lines should be replaced often—sometimes after a single day's fishing. So, buy a good fly line and take care of it.

Leader selection is equally important. A lightweight, tapered leader designed for presenting a small dry fly delicately simply won't turn over a large bass bug. Unless you know precisely what you're after, buying tapered leaders from a tackle shop is pretty much a waste of money; most tapered leaders are designed to suit the needs of trout fishermen. Bluegill anglers can get by with store-bought leaders and can usually find something heavy enough to turn over a size-8 cork bug. In fact, a 6- or 7-foot length of 8- or 10-pound monofilament will usually work. Bass bugs are another matter. The best bet is to tie your own tapered leaders from spools of leader material or monofilament mill-ends. This is very easy, and anyone who can tie an ordinary clinch knot won't have any trouble.

Various gadgets for attaching the leader to the fly line are available, but in my opinion none of these work as nicely as the old nail knot, which is what I recommend for bass angling. I've never trusted those little barbed eyelets that stick into the end of the fly line. Sometimes bass anglers will hook into a large fish in heavy cover, which is a good deal different from hooking a fish on the salt flats or in a trout stream. Sometimes you have to turn a bass instead of letting him run—a lot of strain for those tiny barbs to endure.

You can spend a lot of money on tapered lines and leaders, but for less than $10 you can purchase a good level fly line and all the monofilament leader material you'll need for 20 years. Further, I guarantee that it will work for making casts of normal length with bass bugs of ordinary size.

FLY LINES

The first fly lines were made of braided horsehair. Silk was a great improvement, but today such synthetic materials as nylon and Dacron dominate the market. These excellent modern lines require little care, whereas older lines had to be dressed frequently and thoroughly dried after each fishing trip. Fly fishermen never had it so good!

Modern fly lines are usually classified according to their density, taper, and weight (or size).

DENSITY

Some fly lines float; others sink. Some are even designed to float or sink (*intermediate lines*, they're called), depending on whether or not they're treated with line dressing. And some sinking lines sink faster than others, usually at a predetermined rate measured in inches per second, to allow anglers to fish deeper or shallower water. Some lines have floating bellies and sinking tips. A few even have floating tips and sinking bellies.

But most fly fishing for bass is done with a floating line, even when fishing a few feet down. The plain truth is that floating lines cast easier and better than sinking lines simply because they are easier to pick up from the water. And the higher a line floats, the better I like it. Some of the foamy lines are inherently quite buoyant and float beautifully.

A number of manufacturers market small tins or bottles of paste for dressing a floating line. Most of it is good stuff, but many anglers use far too much of it in an effort to keep their line afloat when what they really need to do is clean their line thoroughly. In time, enough film and dirt can build up to sink the line. I use mild soap and warm water to remove dirt and film. After my line is cleaned and dried, I apply a sparse coat of dressing. A good dressing not only conditions a line but also lubricates it so that it will shoot smoothly through the rod guides.

If you intend to fish deeper than about 5 feet, you'll need a sinking line. You could fish on down with, say, a 10-foot leader on a floating line. As the lure sinks, however, quite a belly develops in the line and leader, making it difficult to detect a pickup and also making it more difficult to set the hook. Moreover, unless the lure is weighted it will sink very slowly—and weighted lures are difficult to cast.

Personally, I prefer a sinking tip or a slow-sinking line when I want to fish from 5 to 10 feet down. For deeper fishing, a fast-sinking line works best. The truth is that deep fishing with a fly rod is rather difficult, but it can be done and will be discussed in more detail in chapter 7.

In most cases, the beginner can get by nicely for a while with a floating line. Later, he can purchase a sinking or sink-tip line and keep it on an extra spool, or perhaps on another reel. Anglers who fish extensively in bassboats often get two complete rigs.

TAPER

I use the term "taper" here only because it's so well established. Bass anglers will do well to think more about how the weight is distributed along the line than about how the diameter changes from one point to another. The beginner should be warned that standard double-tapered line, often called just *tapered* line, is not suitable for casting large bass bugs because the weight is spread evenly along the long belly of the line, and tapered gradually to a fine point on each end—ideal for making fairly short, accurate casts with tiny trout flies. The ideal bassing line *is* tapered, but it's a line with the weight concentrated near the business end, called a *weight-forward line*. Here are the four kinds of fly line as determined by weight distribution and taper:

Level lines, the simplest and least expensive to manufacture, have a uniform diameter from one end to the other. There is no taper, and the weight is evenly distributed. Generally, a level line costs only about 25 percent of the price of a tapered line made of the same material. Because they're economical, level lines are commonly used for bass, bluegills, and other warm-water fish. And they work satisfactorily provided they're matched to the rod and the lure. Long casts can be made with level lines if the lure is light and not too wind-resistant; heavy or highly wind-resistant lures, however, are best cast with a more expensive line designed for the task, especially if you want good distance.

Double-tapered lines have a long, heavy belly with a uniform diameter that tapers down gradually to a light tip at each end. This allows the leader to be attached to either end, meaning the line can be reversed when one end shows signs of wear. Double-tapered line is designed to deliver a small fly with delicacy and finesse. It is not designed to cast heavy bass bugs and large saltwater streamers. I have seen more than one tackle-shop clerk sell a double-tapered line to someone who really needed a level or weight-forward line. Of course, many clerks simply didn't know any better. If you've purchased one of these and don't want to throw it away or use it for trout fishing, cut it in half, tie the small end onto your backing line, and tie your leader onto the big end. If it works for the bugs you're trying to cast you'll have two short lines; if it doesn't work, throw both halves away.

Weight-forward lines have a heavy forward belly tapering gradually to a small tip on the leader end and tapering back quickly to a long length of small-diameter level "shooting" line at the rear end (see the illustration on page 22). Weight-forward line is designed for distance casting with heavy lures, and is ideal for bass fishing. A number of firms market weight-forward lines in special bass-bug or saltwater tapers. These lines feature a much shorter front taper, a shorter, heavier belly, and a shorter rear taper, concentrating line weight near the leader end and easing the task of casting heavier lures into stiff winds. There is some variation from one manufacturer to another and from one weight line to another, but any good weight-forward line handles bugs satisfactorily if the line is matched to the rod and if the bug isn't extravagantly oversized.

Shooting heads, designed for distance casting, are in essence the front 30 or so feet of a weight-forward line attached to a smaller-diameter shooting line. A good shooting head can be made by attaching a shooting line to the first 30 feet of a weight-forward line of suitable weight. Some shooting heads are made with a special shooting line attached (without knots) and some are made with a built-in loop for tying on the shooting line. The shooting line itself can be monofilament (usually about 20-pound test) or a floating braided line.

A shooting taper may save the day when long casts are required, as when one is stalking bass in clear, shallow water, or when jump fishing for schooling bass. Normally, however, a shooting head isn't required in bass angling. In any case, a shooting head offers no advantages unless the angler is an experienced fly caster who knows how to handle the coiled shooting line.

For bass anglers who want to try deep-structure fishing with a fly rod, fast-sinking lead-core shooting heads are available that get flies down fast.

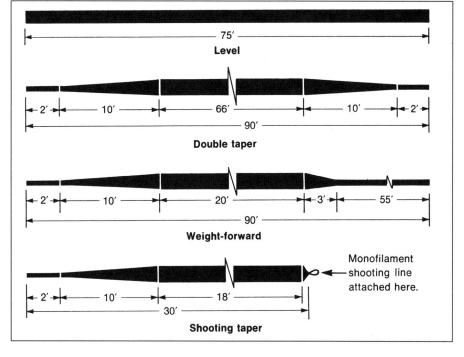

Fly-line tapers and configurations— actual dimensions vary from one brand to another. (Courtesy Scientific Anglers)

WEIGHT

Weight is the most basic consideration in the choice of a fly line, not whether it floats or sinks, or whether it's tapered or level. A fly line that is too light simply won't carry a bass bug. If the line is heavier than necessary, it will overload the rod and tire the angler.

The following table is based on a classification system worked out some time ago by the American Fishing Tackle Manufacturers' Association:

LINE NUMBER	WEIGHT (IN GRAINS)	TOLERANCE RANGE
3	100	94–106
4	120	114–126
5	140	134–146
6	160	152–168
7	185	177–193
8	210	202–218
9	240	230–250
10	280	270–290
11	330	318–342
12	380	368–392

Note that the weight is based on the first 30 feet of line, including the tapered end. The important thing to remember when buying modern gear is not the weight in grains but the assigned number. A rod manufacturer, for example, will specify a 6-weight line for a particular rod and a 9-weight for another. The manufacturer's recommendation will usually be about right, but some leeway is possible, depending in part on the particular angler's style of casting.

The classification of fly lines according to density, taper, and weight (or size) is not really difficult, as I hope I've made clear. Even after you understand the classification system, you might be stumped when first confronted with all the pertinent information jammed together in code in a catalog or on a line's label. I knew one seasoned bass fly-rodder who never understood the business, couldn't read a label, and relied on his sales clerk to guide him through his line selection. Fortunately, he had a sales clerk who knew his stuff and outfitted him with workable albeit expensive lines and leaders. But be warned that in bass-fishing gear you don't always get what you pay for. I once saw a kit for bass anglers in a major mail-order catalog that featured a double-tapered line!

The line-weight code isn't complicated if you understand fly lines and take a few seconds to puzzle it out. Fly lines made in this country (and most made abroad) are coded by taper, weight (size), and type (density), as for example L-9-F. The first part of the code designates the taper (L = level). The middle digit designates the size or weight. The last part designates the type (F = floating). Here's the key:

TAPER	SIZE (OR WEIGHT)	TYPE (DENSITY)
L = level	3 = 100 grains	F = floating
DT = double taper	4 = 120 grains	S = sinking
WF = weight-forward	etc. (see previous	SM = medium sinking
ST = shooting taper	table for line numbers,	SF = fast sinking
	typical weights, and	SXF = extra-fast
	sinking tolerance ranges)	FS = sinking tip
		I = intermediate

Thus, a WF-9-F line would be a weight-forward 9-weight floating line. Some of the old fly-fishing texts list the lines in letters of the alphabet, such as D, for a level line; HDH, for a double-tapered line; or GBF, for a weight-forward line. This system measured diameter, not weight, and thus was of little use in matching line to rod; one manufacturer's HDH might correspond to a 6-weight, another's to a 7-weight, and yet another's to a 5-weight. Thankfully this system is now obsolete.

LEADERS

One reason for using a leader is that it is less visible to fish than a heavy fly line; another is that the leader permits a more gentle presentation of the lure. Visibility and presentation are important in bass angling, though not usually as critical as in trout fishing. Yet leader design is actually more important when casting heavy bugs than when casting dainty dry flies. Visibility aside, the leader is the vital link between a bass angler's line and bug; a limp leader simply will not work. A 9-foot length of 6-pound monofilament, for example, just won't turn over a bug; more often than not the bug falls short of the mark amid a coil of leader. A single length of 20-pound monofilament would work better, but such a heavy tippet is readily visible and can kill the action of light lures. What you need is a tapered leader with a heavy butt and a light tippet.

For most bass fishing, I normally tie a leader about 7 or 8 feet long, or a little shorter than the fly rod I'm using. If I want a 7-foot leader tapered for a 9-weight fly line, I'll usually use about 4 feet of 25-pound monofilament, 1½ feet of 17-pound, and 1½ feet of 10-pound tippet. If I want a 6-pound tippet, I merely tie 8 inches or so to the 10-pound. It may be better to step down in 5-pound increments, maybe with 3 feet of 25-pound, 1½ feet of 20, 1½ feet of 15, and 1 foot of 10. But I try to keep my leaders simple in order to reduce the number of knots required.

The main thing about a bass-fishing leader is that the butt must be stiff enough to turn over the bug. Usually, 25-pound-test monofilament is about right for a 9-weight line, but I usually go up to a 30-pound with a 10-weight line and (usually) down to 20-pound with an 8-weight line. If I seem to be overworking the word "usually" and seem wishy-washy about this leader business, it's because I can't state flatly that 25-pound-test monofilament should be used for the butt end of a leader for a 9-weight fly line. Too much depends on the brand of monofilament, the bug or fly to be cast, and the particular fly line. It is better to proceed empirically.

To avoid compounding the problems of leader design, be sure to stick with the same brand of monofilament for all sections of the leader, except possibly for a short tippet made from a very limp line. The reason is that some monofilament lines are stiffer than others, and it is therefore entirely possible to have a 15-pound midsection that is stiffer than a 25-pound butt!

Anyhow, the important thing to remember when tying leaders for casting heavy lures is that the butt should be almost as stiff as the fly line. Then the stiffness should soften gradually on down to the tippet. Don't forget that stiffness and stiffness alone is the key to designing workable leaders for casting heavy lures, and, unfortunately, neither line diameter nor pound-test rating necessarily reflects stiffness. For this reason, I've always felt that anglers who use precision micrometers in tying leaders are just kidding themselves, unless visibility is their main interest.

For butts I rather like the hard, stiff monofilament leader material made by Mason (Orvis Big Game leader material is similar). But I do tie a short tippet made of softer monofilament onto this special leader line; a stiff tippet can kill the action of a bug or a streamer. It's difficult to find hard monofilament in tackle shops these days because the trend has been toward softer lines to accommodate baitcasting reels as well as spinning reels, but it is available from some of the mail-order houses, of which there are too many to list. Pick up a fly-fishing magazine and order some catalogs.

Regardless of choice of monofilament, I join one length to another with the common blood knot. This is pretty much like two clinch knots, and I have never had one slip on me after I drew it down.

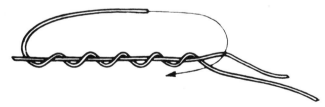

The blood knot

1. Overlap ends of lines to be joined by about 6 inches. Hold at midpoint. Wrap the lines as shown, holding in the middle with your fingers as needed. I recommend at least five turns, as when tying a clinch knot. Repeat the process with the other end of the leader.

2. Note that tag ends point in opposite directions.

3. Pull standing lines slowly in opposite directions, snugging down the knot. Trim off tag ends.

The butt end of the leader is attached to the fly line with a nail knot, at least in my book. As mentioned earlier, several firms sell little barbed metal eyelets that stick into the core of the fly line. I seldom use these, partly because I don't trust them and partly because I don't think they turn over a large bug as well as a nail knot. Still other people swear by some quick-change loop system to attach leaders to fly lines. I don't care for them simply because two loops are larger and heavier than a nail knot. Further, I don't think they transmit the energy from the fly line to the leader as well as a nail knot. I don't have detailed engineering data on the mechanics of the turnover, but I like to think about these things.

The nail knot

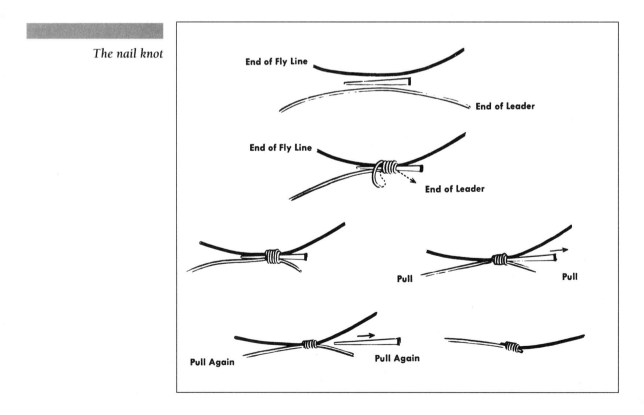

On the other end of the leader, I always tie on the bug or fly with an improved clinch knot. More modern anglers may prefer the uniknot, which is now recommended in some texts and in how-to booklets. Back in the 1970s, I ran an article in *Bass Fishing News* (a tabloid I was publishing for serious bass anglers) about a new uniknot and uniknot "system," which included variations on the basic knot. I fished with the uniknot off and on for about two years, but I switched back to the clinch and improved clinch knot at about the time when many anglers were going to the uniknot. Despite modern arguments to the contrary, I think the clinch knot is easier to tie and is just as strong, but my opinion may be influenced by *long* habit. Suit yourself.

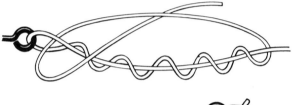

Improved clinch knot for joining leader tippet to fly or hook

The Palomar knot became popular for a while. I don't like the way the thing looks when it's drawn down and I have not used it extensively. Other anglers swear that it's better than the improved clinch knot, or did for a while. Some expert fishermen insist that some sort of loop in the end of the leader should be used with some flies. There are various loop knots, including a variation of the uniknot, but I can't recommend them for most fishing. They do come in handy when working a streamer or bucktail on a heavy shock leader. The loop, of course, permits the lure to be more active. My problem is that I simply don't trust the loop to hold the fish. Of course, the loop will usually tighten up and the knot will hold instead of slipping, but, frankly, I want to draw down my own knots (that's one of the small pleasures of angling). When bass fishing, I'm usually casting to banks and log jams and heavy cover instead of riding around the salt flats. Because it's best to have the bug as close as possible to the cover, hangups are frequent—at least for me. When I try to pull a bug off a log, the knot usually slips down so that I have to retie the knot (using up part of my tippet) if I want the loop. It's just too much trouble.

The Palomar knot

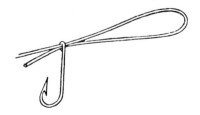

1. Double end of line and run through hook eyelet.

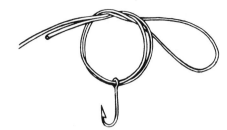

2. Tie overhand knot in doubled line.

3. Pull the loop down and over the hook. Pull tag end and standing line to tighten down knot. Trim.

Flies tied on hooks with turned-down eyes seem to work better with an improved turle knot, which gives the line a straight pull. I haven't illustrated this knot simply because bass anglers seldom use dry flies or other lures with turned-down hook eyes.

If you don't want to tie your own leaders, you can purchase either hand-tied leaders or machine-made knotless tapered leaders. If you shop around carefully, you can find a wide range of leaders from which to choose. Most of these ready-made leaders are classified according to a numbering system, keyed to butt diameter, tippet diameter, and tippet pound test. There is some variation from one brand to another, but the following table is typical:

SIZE	BUTT DIAMETER (IN INCHES)	TIPPET DIAMETER (IN INCHES)	POUND TEST
3X	0.021	0.008	4
2X	0.021	0.009	5
1X	0.023	0.010	6
0X	0.023	0.011	7
9/5	0.025	0.012	10
8/5	0.025	0.013	12
7/5	0.029	0.014	14

Many store-bought tapered leaders come with a loop on the butt end. As I said, I don't care for these, but, admittedly, loops make it easy to change from one leader to another. Personally, I seldom change a whole leader, and I have fished for months with the same butt. I do, however, frequently change my tippet. This, in turn, soon inches away at the next link in the leader until it's too short and has to be replaced or extended.

Whether you purchase tapered leaders or tie your own, it's advisable to take proper care of them, especially if you're using a light tippet in lunker country. Inspect the tippet and smaller portions of the leader frequently. Nicks and abrasions often can be detected by running the line (under slight tension) between thumb and forefinger. Don't keep spare leaders or leader materials in sunlight; ultraviolet rays weaken monofilament.

Check your leader frequently for wind knots. These simple overhand knots can weaken monofilament line by as much as 50 percent.

Monofilament has what is called "memory." If coiled for any length of time, monofilament tends to return to the same coiled shape when you're casting and fishing with it. Stretching the leader before a fishing trip helps, but the best cure for memory is to rub the leader between rubber surfaces. Just cut a small piece of inner tube, fold it over between thumb and forefinger, and pull the line through it.

BACKING LINE

Fly reels with large-diameter spools will accommodate quite a lot of backing line. Whether or not you expect to tie into a large fish, you should install the correct amount of backing line so that the fly line fills the spool. A full spool not only ensures a faster pickup and retrieve but also reduces line coil.

Determining the exact amount of backing line is best done by first spooling on the fly line, leader end first. Then attach the backing line with a nail knot and fill the spool within ⅛ inch or so of capacity. Next, tie the end of the backing line temporarily to a tree and walk off until you've stripped all the line from the reel. Then tie the end of the backing line to the reel arbor and respool. I attach the backing line (or the fly line if no backing line is used) to the spool as shown in the accompanying illustration.

Any sort of backing line of suitable strength will do, but most experienced fly

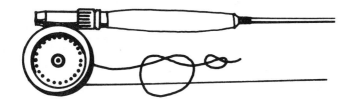

Fastening backing to reel

fishermen prefer 20-pound Dacron, which is long lived and stretches very little. Any braided line will work, and some anglers use monofilament. If you do use monofilament, remember that it stretches; if spooled under tension, it can exert enough pressure to damage your reel spool.

Finally, the nail knot connecting the backing line to the fly line should be smooth so that it won't hang in one of the rod guides, which could someday cause you to lose a big fish. Tying the knot carefully, drawing it down slowly, and trimming it closely will help. It also helps to apply a drop of Pliobond or similar pliable cement.

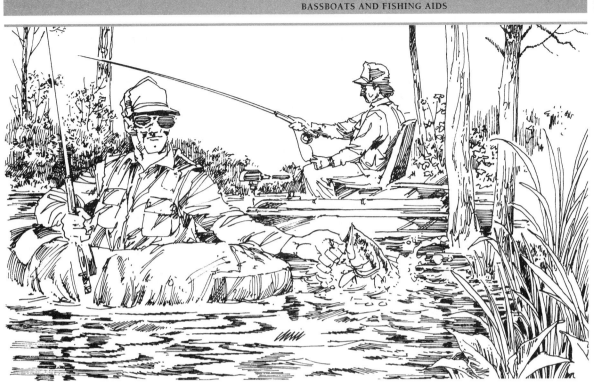

CHAPTER 4

BASSBOATS AND FISHING AIDS

The development of the bassboat is the greatest thing to happen to the sport since the invention of the rod and reel. And the worst. I haven't checked the *Guinness Book of Records*, but I read somewhere that a bassboat on an impoundment in Tennessee was clocked at 92.045 miles per hour. I wasn't on it, but I can talk about the subject from experience.

On the St. Johns. Skimming over the smooth waters of a cove in a large lake on the St. Johns River at 71 miles per hour on my partner's bassboat wasn't too bad. I had just begun to enjoy the ride and nod to the blue herons that cocked their heads from a narrow border of green grass to watch us streak by. I wasn't ready for the whitecaps when we rounded the point and headed into the choppy waters on the main lake.

"Hold the rods! Hold the rods!" the guy yelled, gunning the boat. To hell with the rods. I locked onto the boat seat with both hands.

A successful businessman from Atlanta, he had seemed sensible enough the night before when we were planning our strategy for the first day of the tournament. It wasn't until he got behind the boat's steering wheel at the starting line, revved up the big outboard motor, and lowered his goggles that I saw the unmistakable gleam in his eye. Too late. The gun sounded. Off we went, racing for our fishing hole 20 miles upriver.

On the Arkansas. During my next tournament, near Little Rock, my first-day partner was a Cajun from Baton Rouge. Following a hot tip from a local angler, he thought the bass fishing would be better 34 miles up the river, although I told him that the tournament would be won at the wing dams almost within the city limits of Little Rock (which turned out to be the case). But we headed upstream at full throttle, right on the tail of another tournament fisherman, a cowboy from Texas. We were skimming the slick waters of the Arkansas when a tugboat and barge appeared in a river bend up ahead. When we hit their wake, the cowboy panicked and cut his engine. I sat speechless, rigid as an "L" in my seat, as our boat topped the wave and soared 10 feet through the air before coming down hard—within inches of the first boat. Unshaken, the Cajun gunned the motor and skimmed on up the Arkansas as if nothing had happened. As best I could decipher his remarks over the roar of the huge outboard, he felt that we had scored a major victory by getting out in front of the competition. To hell with the competition.

In Georgia. I don't quit easily. Six months after the Arkansas event I ended up in a boat with a Tallahassee motor mechanic on Lake Seminole, Georgia. Fast boats were his thing, and I knew he was going to run despite a cold front that had moved in the night before the tournament. At the crack of day it was 18 degrees and windy. Considering the boat speed, the chill factor must have been 100 degrees below zero.

I had on five layers of clothing, but I knew it wasn't enough as soon as we blasted off. We had on crash helmets and windshields, but it was too cold to look dead ahead, although I could feel us leaning to port or starboard as we maneuvered through hundreds of acres of standing timber. I still don't know how that hotrod managed to run the channel at that speed in that weather. Maybe we were just very lucky. I didn't freeze to death, but I still have a touch of bursitis from time to time to remind me of it.

After the Seminole event, I began to consider the merits of bass fishing from an old wooden boat within easy casting distance of a bank with lots of stumps and cypress knees and lily pads. It's a pleasure to cast to such cover whether you catch a fish or not.

But a lot can be said for the bassboat as a movable fishing platform that is easy to keep in casting position. The most important feature, in my opinion, is a bow-mounted electric motor. These are often called trolling motors, but not many people actually troll with them. The purpose of the motor is to keep the boat in casting position, and the bow mount works better than a transom mount simply because it's easier to control a boat's direction by pulling it than by pushing it.

To me, this feature is even more important when fly-rodding from a boat than when using a baitcasting or spinning rig. Anyone who has ever worked an irregular shoreline with bass bugs for eight hours from a 12-foot aluminum jonboat with slat seats, or from a canoe with a paddle in one hand and a fly rod in the other, will know exactly what I mean.

Most bass anglers prefer remote-controlled motors, which have a foot pedal for remote starting and stopping and controlling the direction of thrust, leaving both hands free for fishing. Some anglers prefer to eliminate the cumbersome foot pedal and use a manually steered motor, but this rig requires steering by hand or by nudging it with a foot or knee. The choice is yours. Personally, I feel more in control of things with my foot on the pedal.

An easily controlled electric motor is also a help when battling a large fish. I can quickly swing the bow of the boat around one way or the other to help prevent a fish from getting under the boat, and I always head the boat away from the cover when I tie into a large bass with a light tippet. I once caught a long, skinny 7-pound largemouth while fishing for bluegills and, to make a long story short, I don't think I would have landed the fish if I hadn't been able to work the boat away from the bank with the electric motor.

Modern electric motors are available in 12- or 24-volt models. For large boats, 24-volts works best; for average-size craft, 12-volt motors will do. Most bass anglers use deep-cycle marine batteries, but ordinary car batteries will work just fine and have served me well in times of famine. When I first got married and bought a house on an island in Florida's Lake Weir, unexpected lawyer's fees and closing costs put us on a tight budget. My bride and I had a jonboat rigged with an electric fishing motor, which we powered by taking the battery out of our car and putting it into the boat. (That's how short money was.) Many times, when we wanted (or needed) a few fish for supper, we would go out with the paddle instead of bothering to remove the battery from the car. This worked pretty well after my wife learned how to hold the boat an exact distance from the bank. By the time our first anniversary came around, I gave her a new 12-volt marine battery so that she wouldn't have to paddle the jonboat anymore in her condition. Well, her reaction wasn't what I had expected, to say the least. I concluded that there's simply no way to understand women.

Anyhow, I believe that a foot-controlled electric motor has at least doubled my catch of bass, and could well have tripled it.

A full-fledged bassboat is fitted with an electronic depthfinder (discussed later), and has pedestal-mounted swiveling easy seats instead of rock-hard slat seats. Available in varying degrees of comfort, the seats should swivel freely so the angler can face the target without having to twist about. If you like to stand up to cast, consider a boat with elevated fishing decks and removable pedestal seats, some of which can be lifted out of a socket in seconds and be put back in just as quickly, or they can be folded back for running. Most bassboats have a steering console, but a few are operated directly from low-mounted fishing seats, either by manually steering a kicker on the stern or with some sort of stick steering mechanism up front. These seats can be dangerous, and no passenger should be allowed to ride in deck-mounted fishing seats while the boat is underway. If the boat hits something, swirls, or slows drastically, anyone in the pedestal seat will be thrown head over heels.

From the outset, the trend has been toward larger bassboats, and today a fully rigged boat can cost more than a car. They're worth the money if you do a lot of fishing on big water and can afford such a boat, but look around carefully before buying, and make certain that you get a boat that suits your needs. There are many combinations of bass and ski boats, or family boats, if you're so inclined and want to help justify the big purchase. If you plan to fish in the bass tournaments, you'll want a large, fast rig with two large live wells and a big motor so that you can move about without wasting time. But if you don't fish tournaments, a smaller kicker and one live well will do fine. If you release your catch, you won't need even a single live well. In fact, if you want to keep a few fish for the table it's a good idea to keep them in an ice chest instead of in a live well. On small boats, I've kept plenty of fish on stringers, but an ice chest works better in my opinion.

If you're interested in bassboats but don't know exactly what you need, your best bet is to attend a large boat show or visit several dealers to get some idea of what's available.

As versatile as a bassboat may be, don't mistake it for a heavy-weather boat designed for the open ocean. I used to work for Lew Childre, the man who revolutionized bass-fishing tackle, and once he went out to fish for a few hours in Mobile Bay on a well-known fiberglass bassboat made in Arkansas. A squall came up and Lew almost didn't make it back in. The next day he put some people to work building a wooden bassboat, following a design used by old-time commercial fishermen in the Mobile Bay area. It had a V-bow, a bilge, wooden deck, steering wheel, swivel chairs, fishing motor, two depthfinders—the works. The boat wouldn't win a race, but it was a wonderful fishing platform. After trying it out on the lower Apalachicola, fishing from the bay to the cypress sloughs upstream, Lew told me that he would never again go fishing in an Arkansas hog trough.

MINI-BASSBOATS AND OTHER OPTIONS

The bassboat principle—bow-mounted electric motor, depthfinder, and comfortable fishing seats that swivel—can be adapted to other kinds of boats, such as the popular jonboat. A small deck or some sort of bracket will have to be installed up front so that the electric motor can be mounted. Since motors of different models have different mounting mechanics, it's best to know exactly which kind of electric you'll be using. The depthfinder can be mounted on the bow so that you can see it

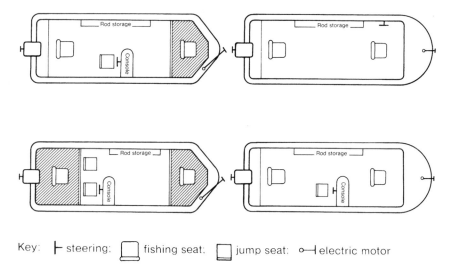

Key: ⊢ steering; ▢ fishing seat: ▢ jump seat: ⚬⊣ electric motor

easily while fishing or while running the boat. The transducer can be mounted on the shaft of the electric motor, but in this case it will not be in the water and functioning while the boat is underway. One alternative is to mount the transducer back toward the rear of the boat, then connect it to a bow-mounted monitor. (Remember that the transducer must be mounted on the part of the hull that is in contact with the water, or else it must be mounted outside the hull. In any case, transducer placement can be tricky, so read the manufacturer's instructions carefully.) On jonboats, swivel seats usually can be mounted on the slat seats. I've also seen larger jonboats fitted with a plywood deck on the bow, making a platform for mounting a pedestal seat, electric motor, and depthfinder monitor. These may work on larger jonboats, but remember that the elevated deck and the pedestal seat tend to make the boat top-heavy and dangerous. Never ride in such a seat while the boat is underway.

A bow-mounted electric motor and depthfinder can be fitted to canoes, although canoes are not as stable as jonboats. I once fished successfully from a 14-foot square-sterned canoe by mounting a clamp-on electric motor on the rear. A portable depthfinder, which contained its own battery, was mounted on the deck, and a transducer was attached to the shaft of the electric motor. Remember that a 12-volt battery and an electric motor add a lot of weight to a canoe. If you put all this stuff and a fisherman on the same end, you'll have the other end sticking up into the air.

When rigging any boat, remember that you'll need a battery and electrical wires running to and from the electric motor, wires to and from the depthfinder, and a cable to connect depthfinder to transducer. All this stuff can get in the way and can trip you up. Of course, it's especially bad for the fly fisherman who keeps lots of line off the reel. Consequently, it's best to figure out ways to clamp or otherwise contain all the wires on either side of the boat, out of the way.

Some very nice—even deluxe—one- and two-man mini-bassboats are available. These have comfortable swivel seats and are designed to mount an electric motor on the bow. Typically, these craft are rather wide but short—4 by 8 feet, or shorter, squared off on both ends. (If you're buying, be sure to get one that fits nicely into the back of your pickup truck.) Some will take a small outboard, but for small waters the bow-mounted electric motor is all you'll need. These craft are ideal for fishing small farm ponds and quiet coves of larger lakes and impoundments. They will also work in slow-moving streams, but they tend to bounce around in swift water and are hard to control.

On the one-man mini-bassboats, a swivel seat is located more or less in the center of the craft. This is ideal because it makes the boat more stable. Usually, the seat is mounted over a battery storage compartment, which also aids stability. On the two-man boats, the seats are too close together, making it difficult for two people to fly fish at the same time, unless they're quite compatible. Sometimes sitting back to back works pretty well.

FLOAT TUBES

Of course, you don't need a boat to catch bass in small lakes, farm ponds, and most streams. In fact, a large boat in some waters will scare the fish half to death. Truck-size inner tubes fitted with a fabric cover and seat, called *float tubes* or *belly boats,* split the difference between wading and fishing from a boat.

Round float tubes have been around quite a while, and have always been difficult to get in and out of. More recently, U-shaped float tubes have begun appearing, and are much easier to enter and exit; you just back up to the floating tube and sit down. U-shaped float tubes are also faster through the water, and some anglers feel that they're more comfortable. A U-shaped float tube typically sells for about twice the price of a round float tube, however. Float tubes of either type are available with various tackle and gear compartments sewn into the fabric covers, and most have stripping aprons to keep slack fly line in check and air-filled backrests to provide emergency flotation.

In cool weather, or when fishing a cold-water stream, most tubing anglers wear chest waders to keep dry. Some tubers propel themselves with a small paddle, but I think it's best to wear rubber flapper-type swimfins or special tube fins made of metal. The latter are fitted with hinges so that the fin straightens out when the foot moves forward; on the back stroke, the fin hinges back 90 degrees, thereby creating forward thrust. It's rather like walking through the water.

In addition to their logical role as a highly portable aid to fishing ponds and lakes, tubes are often used in wading streams. Normally, the angler keeps his feet on the bottom, but uses the tube to drift over deep holes.

In any case, the bass angler should also consider the following fishing aids:

Depthfinders. In my opinion, no bassboat is complete without at least one depthfinder aboard. Many anglers, myself included, like to use a second depthfinder. The main depthfinder operates when the boat is running at high speed. Its transducer is most often mounted toward the rear of the boat, and the monitor is usually mounted on the steering console. The second depthfinder is mounted forward, with the monitor near the bow and the transducer on the shaft of the electric motor.

Portable depthfinders are available, but I prefer permanently mounted units because they don't bounce around, and because they operate from the boat's 12-volt battery system instead of internal batteries.

Depthfinders have made great strides since they were first introduced. First came flasher units, which indicated depth by a flashing light. The expert could determine whether they were over hard or soft bottom by how brightly the light flashed; flashes between the bottom and the surface indicated fish, or at least so went the theory. After these became old hat, some bass anglers started using chart recorders, which traced a profile of the bottom, and whatever was suspended above it (fish), on slowly moving chart paper. Then came inexpensive LCD (Liquid Crystal Diode) units, which have a screen display similar to a laptop computer or a fancy digital watch. The best of these are said to be able to distinguish among fish species, and show fish shapes right on the screen. Innovations continue, and units that look forward and sideways as well as down are now available, as well as units that incorporate Loran electronic navigation units, chart plotters, and GPS. Although the units are sometimes called *fish finders,* and will indeed show fish on the monitor, the main purpose of the depthfinder—at least for bass fishing—is to show the depth of the water and perhaps something of the bottom contour and "structure."

Although the fly-rodder usually fishes in rather shallow water, depthfinders are still very helpful. If, for example, you're fishing the shoreline or visible cover in a submerged creek bottom of a manmade impoundment, you'll be more likely to catch a large bass where the old creek channel runs close to cover. So whether or not you fish in it, you need to know where the creek channel is—an easy task for a depthfinder. When you cross the creek channel, the depthfinder indicates a dip followed by a rise. An expert can estimate the width of the creek channel and the slope of the banks, and can sometimes tell something about what's on the bottom.

Most problems with new depthfinder installations can be traced to an improperly mounted transducer. Cavitation or air bubbles from the boat's hull, or electrical interference from the outboard, can cause erratic signals, and can even cause the signals to disappear from the dial. During the past few years, most of these problems have been worked out by manufacturers and boat riggers. To ensure dependable service, follow the manufacturer's instructions as closely as possible.

Temperature indicators. At one time, hand-held temperature indicators were popular with some bass anglers. Basically, a weighted probe was lowered into the water on color-coded line; the temperature appeared on a dial, and the color-coded line indicated the depth of the reading. This system was too much trouble and took too long, however, and most modern bass fishermen who are interested in temperature now mount continuous-reading surface-temperature meters on their bassboats; these can give readings while the boat is running across the lake, and they're very convenient for determining temperature at the surface. Of course, this doesn't provide much of a clue to the temperature on the bottom.

Light meters are hand-held units that work similarly to temperature probes. Light meters have limited application to fly fishing, and, frankly, I've never used mine while I was after bass. I have, however, experimented with it from time to time, and I feel that I am a more knowledgeable angler for it. (Some results of my efforts are set forth in chapter 10.) As an on-site tool, however, the light meter is just too much trouble because it has to be lowered and raised by hand.

Oxygen monitors. I once owned an oxygen monitor, or probe, and I feel that I learned some things from it. For example, I once caught a large bass from the bottom of a 35-foot hole near my home, and thereafter I spent many hours fishing there for another one. When I obtained an oxygen monitor, I made a quick check and was surprised to see that there wasn't enough oxygen on the bottom to support bass. After that, I used the oxygen monitor for a year or so when I wanted to fish the hole, or some similar spot. If the oxygen was low, I moved on. If the oxygen level was right, I fished with more confidence. But the oxygen monitor soon conked out on me. I never replaced it, and I never will.

pH meters are similar to oxygen monitors—and a good deal of magazine and book ink has been used in their praise, and in finding water where the pH is exactly right. I've never gone for one of these for the same reason that I didn't replace my oxygen monitor.

Color analyzers. Believe it or not, these are probes that measure depth and light intensity, then feed the information into a tiny hand-held analog computer. A dial shows the color of the lure to use for the prevailing conditions. Some lure manufacturers even got on the bandwagon and offered lures that fitted into such a scheme. The truth as I see it is that the size and the action of a lure is far more important in bass fishing than color. This is especially true of popping bugs and other surface lures.

The bottom line, I think, is that anyone who fishes in impoundments, and, to a lesser extent, in a large natural lake or stream, can really benefit from a good depthfinder. The other gadgets are just that, although I might add that some very important outdoor writers and TV show hosts have held other opinions in the past. What the future holds, nobody knows. I thought 15 years ago that I had seen everything, but now I'm beginning to wonder. I don't think bass anglers ought to be blind to new products, but I do think they ought to realize that we already have the greatest fish-finding system ever devised. I'm talking about a good rod, reel, line, and lure. If a bass takes a lure, you'll know that fish are present, and that water temperature, light intensity, oxygen level, and pH are right for fish.

In any case, here are a few more fishing aids that need to be covered:

Maps. A contour map of a lake or impoundment can be invaluable to a bass angler. A good hydrologic map or nautical chart will help, and detailed topographic maps can be obtained for many areas from the U.S. Geological Survey. To obtain information about maps of specific impoundments, write to the Map Information Office, U.S. Geological Survey National Center, 12201 Sunrise Valley Drive, Reston, Virginia 22092. Be certain to mention that you are interested in fishing the impoundment and would therefore need a map showing manmade structure as well as contour lines. In some cases, new topographic maps might not show such features, so that, if available, copies of older maps are much more useful. Commercial contour maps and guidebooks are available for some lakes and impoundments.

Although I don't recommend fly fishing submerged structures in more than 25 feet of water, you should be thoroughly familiar with the water depth of a lake or impoundment. Quite often bass, especially larger ones, will be in cover or structure near deep water, and a good contour map can help locate these areas near deep water.

County road maps that show some of the secondary roads often missing on highway maps or travel atlases can help locate bridges across the creeks and draws of impoundments. Bridges often provide good fishing. More often than not the banks of the bridge approaches will be covered with riprap—good places to fish either from a small boat or from the bank.

Waders. Although I've waded around the edges of some lakes and some streams in nothing but jeans and sneakers, I feel better using chest-high waders. Some of these have boot feet attached; others have stocking feet and are intended for wearing under a separate set of shoes, boots, or sandals. Strap-on devices with cleats or other special gripping aids are available. I prefer boot waders with felt soles. In addition to its nonslip properties, felt permits you to move quietly. Whichever sort of waders you choose, buy good ones and take care of them.

Hip boots will do for very shallow wading, but I usually end up getting wet when I use them. Frankly, I believe that, if you should step into deep or swift water, hip boots are much more dangerous than waders. Waders are pretty safe, provided you wear a belt around them at the waist to prevent them from quickly filling with water. With hip boots, there's nothing to prevent them from filling. On the other hand, it is easier to get out of hip boots.

Fishing vests. Wading all day in a stream without a good fishing vest is almost like hiking overnight without a good backpack. Modern fishing vests have pockets all over them, inside and out, with pockets on pockets and under pockets, and will hold an amazing amount of tackle, leaders, flies, insect repellent, and the like. For short trips up or down a stream, however, a vest isn't necessary for bass fishing, and is often too hot. Extra tippet material, clippers, and a few bugs or streamers are all one needs. Cliché or not, I put extra bugs and flies on my straw hat.

Although the biggest danger on most streams is falling down in very shallow water, anglers unaccustomed to wading may be uneasy about getting in over their heads. If so, I suggest that they look into flotation vests with pockets.

Tackle boxes. Streamers and bucktails can be kept in fly books, which have "pages" of felt, wool, or some similar material that holds the hook's point without dulling it. Although these books work fine with even large streamers and bucktails, they are not ideal for bugs and such flies as the muddler, which have more body and tend to get mashed.

Bass bugs—especially those with rubber legs on either side—are best kept in compartments. Plastic boxes designed to hold such things are available, but frankly I prefer an ordinary tackle box with wide compartments. I have some very large bugs with rubber legs that I don't like to squeeze into a small place. If you do most of your fishing from a boat, I'd advise you to get a large tackle box so that you'll have plenty of room for extra reel spools, tippet material, and so on. Then, if you should wade a stream, you can get out only what you think you'll need.

If you fish with soft plastic worms and other such lures, be sure to get a box that's "worm proof." Worm material will melt or "burn" some plastic boxes. And be sure to keep your worms separate—isolated—unless you want your pretty flies and bugs to end up a sticky, wretched mess. Plastic-worm bags are highly advisable.

Landing nets. I seldom use a landing net for bass. Instead, I work them up close and grasp the lower jaw with thumb and forefinger. If you do use a landing net, get one that's big enough, and don't try to scoop up a lunker bass with a net that's narrower than the fish is long. I've caught a number of bass over 26 inches long, which means that a 30-inch net wouldn't be too large. More bass, I'd say, have been lost during the last moments of the battle than at any other time simply because the excited angler, or his fishing companion, tried to scoop them up in a small net. I also recommend a net with wide mesh, and one made from green or brown nylon cording. A white net suddenly stuck into the water, or swatted down, will sometimes scare a lunker bass into one last lunge, and this can be disastrous at close quarters.

In any case, it's best to land your own lunker without help from a fishing partner. At least, that's the way I feel about it.

Stripping baskets. Most fly-rodders keep some line off the reel, and those who shoot for distance keep a lot off. Stepping on this line can ruin it, and tangles can foul up a shooting cast. Instead of having this line loose on the boat deck, or trailing in the water if you're wading, some anglers prefer a stripping basket strapped around the waist with a belt. Such baskets are available from some of the specialty shops and mail-order houses. Some anglers improvise their own by cutting slits for a belt in a small plastic dishpan, and drilling holes in the bottom to let out water. Although stripping baskets can add yards to a cast—especially if you're wading and shooting a lot of line—it's pretty hard to keep a line in a stripping basket consistently. If you aren't careful, part of the line flops over the side, often pulling the rest of the line along with it.

Cameras. Large impoundments have many purposes, including flood control. Typically, the water level rises and falls, depending on rainfall, controlled water usage, and other factors. A log that lies on the beach on one fishing trip might well be submerged on the next, making prime cover for a bass. If you remember such cover or structure in impoundments that you fish often, your catch will surely increase. On large impoundments with a hundred miles of shoreline, most of us need some system of keeping up with such potential hotspots. A camera and a notebook will be a big help, especially if a log or some such cover is shown in relation to an easily recognized feature on the bank above the high-water level. A few years back, Polaroid cameras were ideal for this purpose because they produced instant prints and the angler could make notes on the back. Modern anglers might prefer a hand-held video camera, and those who have everything might mount a videocassette player on their boat's console.

Polarized sunglasses. Besides cutting glare and making the day's outing more pleasant, good polarized sunglasses will help you catch more bass. This is especially true in shallow, clear water. I personally don't think it's sporting to stalk bass when they're bedding, but if you want to try it, polarized glasses will certainly help you spot the beds.

They will also help you keep your eye on your bug, and this can be important. Seeing the bass strike will help you react quicker, and the quicker you react the better will be your chances of setting the hook.

ll manner of bugs and streamers and other lures are discussed in the following chapters. At this point I'd like to make a couple of comments that apply to any fly-rod lure. First, most bugs and some flies are sold with hooks that aren't truly sharp. Always inspect the point of a hook, new or old, before fishing with it. The larger the hook, the sharper it should be. Be especially critical of the heavy-duty hooks used for saltwater-type bugs and streamers. There are all manner of gadgets on the market for sharpening hooks, but in my opinion it's hard to beat a small file.

Second, look at the hook eyelet on your balsa and cork bass bugs. Most manufacturers dip their bugs into lacquer, often leaving behind a clogged eyelet. Some firms drill through this paint, leaving a hard, sharp edge that will cut your leader tippet. Always clean all the paint from in and around an eyelet. On old bugs, watch out for rust. A rusty eyelet can abrade the tippet when you draw down the knot.

Third, a lot of bass fishermen err by buying a bug so heavy and wind-resistant that they can't cast it with normal fly gear. In general, I don't recommend any lure—feather, hair, or cork—tied on a hook larger than 1/0.

In the chapters that follow, I have generally avoided the subject of lure color.

PART 2
LURES AND HOW TO FISH THEM

Although it's pretty well established that black bass can distinguish between some colors, and may even prefer one color over another, I believe that hot colors have more to do with the latest TV fishing show or magazine article than with the bass. Maybe I'm wrong, but I find it strange that bass will hit only a motor-oil worm one year and a pumpkinseed worm the next. On the other hand, even skeptics like me will change colors when the fish aren't biting.

Whatever the truth may be, the best bet is to stock up with a variety of colors and switch about until you find something that is hot for the day or that will keep your hopes up until the fish start biting. For openers, you might try light colors in clear water, dark colors in dark water; light colors in shallow water, dark in deep; light during midday, dark early in the morning and late in the afternoon. In any case, look at the bottom of surface lures to see what color you're actually fishing with. The bass don't see all the pretty colors and eyes on the top of a bug unless it turns upside down in the water. Once I was fishing with a fellow who, after a long dry spell, said he thought he'd try a frog pattern. His bug did look rather like a frog on top, but the bottom was plain yellow!

CHAPTER 5

FISHING ON TOP

If I were a poet, I would probably begin this chapter by praising the beauties of a lake or stream at sunrise or sunset, or by painting the picture of a lone angler only vaguely seen on a misty morning—but fishing a bass bug at such times is likely to elicit such an eruption in the calm waters that the fly-rodder will quickly forget to observe the qualities of the day. In my opinion, there is no greater thrill in angling than a bass (or a snook) smashing a surface bug.

Yet bugs and other surface lures aren't always the best bet for taking bass. Most bass caught on a fly rod are, to be sure, hooked on the surface, but this is because that's where most fly-rodders fish. Generally, bass hit surface lures better in early morning, late afternoon, at night, and on cloudy or rainy days. And nearly always in shallow water. A bass will seldom rise from 20 feet down to hit a surface lure, no matter how skillfully it is played. Consequently, the fly-rodder can usually catch a heftier stringer of bass by going deeper during the heat of the day. But there are exceptions, and I've caught 8-pound bass on surface lures at midday in clear water under a bright sun. These exceptions occur just often enough to hold me along a shoreline or grass bed long after I should have headed for deeper waters. The plain truth is that fishing on the surface is more fun. It's also much easier.

Although deer-hair bugs have been around for some time, the first cork bugs were made by E. H. Peckinpaugh in the early 1900s. Most of the popping bugs on the market today are still made from cork, but hard plastic bugs are not uncommon. I prefer balsa bugs over either cork or plastic because they seem to be a little bouncier in the water, but the material doesn't lend itself to mass production and balsa bugs are hard to find in tackle shops. Foam bugs, which have a body molded from closed-cell foam around S-shanked hooks, just as leadhead jigs are molded around dogleg jig hooks, are becoming more common, and molds as well as foam sheets and precut foam popper heads are now readily available for the do-it-yourselfer.

Before discussing the various bug designs, I'd like to point out two basic errors to avoid when selecting a bass bug. First, many bass anglers experienced with hardware but new to fly fishing fail to understand that the larger the bug the harder it is to cast, and they tend to buy large bugs that cannot be cast easily with normal bass rods and line. On the other hand, experienced fly-rodders going after bass for the first time often use bugs that are too small for best results. Second, many bugs on the market— especially those with fat bodies—will not hook fish as often as they should. Remember that a bug's body is fitted around the hook's shank, and this can result in a lure that doesn't have enough "bite." A bug should be made on a long shank hook, and the point should be well behind the end of the bug's body. The hooking properties of an ill-designed bug can be improved by springing the point out a bit to one side, or down, or both ways—but this reduces the hook's holding power.

Unlike trout and salmon flies, bass bugs haven't been endlessly patterned, variegated, named, and cataloged—but the trend has started. Although manufacturers and individual craftsmen like Dave Whitlock and Larry Dahlberg have given names to their creations, the major designs of topwater bugs depend more on the shape of the bug's body than on the various dressings of hair and feathers. Of course it's important that the bug be dressed, but I don't think the bass much care whether the tail feathers are natural badger or dyed olive grizzly.

POPPERS

These highly popular bugs have a hollow, dished-out face designed to cause a pop, or plop, when the angler twitches the rod tip or hauls in line with a little jerk. There is a certain sound to a good popper, and it's the sonic thing that arouses bass. Or so it seems. The popper doesn't merely push water spray ahead, and doesn't merely create a ruckus on the surface of the water. If I see it correctly, the face of

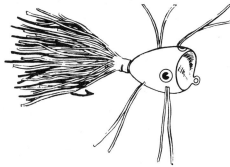

Poppers have a dished-out face. (Courtesy Accardo)

a good popper plunges downward, creating air bubbles and directing a sort of acoustical blast into the water. It is, of course, possible to pop a bug too loudly, and I believe that many bass anglers err in this direction, especially in shallow water. At times a very gentle plop may be required to coax a bass to hit. On the other hand, a popper worked fast and furious will sometimes trigger strikes when all else fails. As a general rule, I pop a bug rather loudly at night or in muddy or stained water, more gently in clear water; loudly in water deeper than 4 or 5 feet, more gently in shallow water.

Popper Splash, a loud-mouthed bug from Accardo (Courtesy Accardo)

Apart from the loudness of the pop, a popper can be fished slow or fast. The question is how long to wait between pops. Erratic retrieves will of course catch bass, but a more studied approach usually works best for me. My favorite method of fishing a popper is first to present it gently on the cast and then wait until the waves dissipate before popping it. Then wait again until the ripples dissipate before making the second pop, and so on for five or six pops. Then pick up and recast to another spot. The reasoning behind this retrieve is that the pops hold the bass's attention and the long pauses play on its curiosity and patience. Another tactic is to twitch the bug slightly. Twitch it again a little harder, then pop it lightly. Then continue with a series of pops that are progressively more vigorous and frequent. The idea behind this retrieve is to convince the bass that the bug has fallen into the water, was stunned, slowly recovers, and makes away. This retrieve can also be used with other surface lures, and has taken many a bass for pluggers.

Popping bugs can be difficult to cast. Weight and air resistance are factors with any bass bug, and poppers further complicate casting because they create a lot of resistance on the pickup. Some even tend to dive. The trick is to start the bug moving along the surface before picking it up; make it take off like an airplane. The actual lift-off shouldn't occur until the rod is at about a 45-degree angle; the elevated rod tip, together with the increasing speed, will make the bug come up smoothly instead of diving or popping. What's more, sliding the bug along the surface will sometimes trigger a strike from a bass that had ignored the pop-and-rest routine. In fact, it's not a bad idea to *fish* the bug during the pickup.

By contrast, some anglers jerk their bugs out of the water, causing enough ruckus to lower their chances of catching a bass on subsequent casts in the vicinity. Not long ago I fished behind such a fellow in a bassboat. We were casting down the edge of a long grass bank late in the afternoon. Quite correctly, he wanted his bug within inches of the grass, or exactly in a foot-wide pocket. But this guy sometimes made three or four casts, slash and thrash, before he got his bug exactly where he wanted it, and each time he made a short cast he immediately snatched the bug out of the water and angrily plopped it back. The more he worked at it, the worse he got. It would have been better (at least for my state of mind) if he had fished out his bum casts instead of frothing the water.

Anyhow, well-fished poppers are great bugs for bass. Big-mouthed poppers are ideal for fishing out pockets in lily pads or for casting to stumps and similar cover. Water resistance prevents the bug from moving far when popped, meaning you can keep the bug in the pocket instead of pulling it out. At the other extreme, poppers aren't ideal for covering a lot of water fast, so that the complete bass fisherman will have other bugs on hand.

I might add here that medium-size poppers will take both bass and bluegills. For bluegills, however, the worst thing you can do with a popping bug is pop it. Bluegills are cautious fish and will often stand off and watch a bug for some time before taking it. A pop will send a bluegill darting off, although it may come back. Anyhow, the way to fish a medium-size bug is to splash it around for bass during the first part of the retrieve, then let it sit perfectly still while you slowly count to 10. This technique is especially effective with poppers that have rubber legs sticking out the sides, which may wiggle a little even when the bug sits still. Bass will also hit while the bug is still, or when you move it again.

PUSHERS

Although some bugs of this type are called poppers and will pop, they don't have hollow faces and don't have quite the same sonic effect. They will create surface bubbles, but they don't trap as much air and direct it downward into the water, and thus may not be as good as poppers for attracting bass from some distance away.

Top row: Popper designs. The bug on the left, without a slanted face, tends to dive. Bottom row: A pusher (left) doesn't have a dished-out face. A slider (middle) has a pointed face. A spouter (right) has a triangulated face.

I usually fish pushers pretty much the same way as poppers, but in a different frame of mind. I think of them as imitations of something (such as a frog) going through the water with steady, stop-and-go, lunging strokes. In any case, pushers can be worked faster than poppers and lend themselves better to a fast, zigzag retrieve.

A lot of pusher bodies are longer and thinner than poppers, but a few, such as the Gerbubble Bug, are flattened instead of rounded. Weight and air resistance being equal, pushers are easier to pick up and therefore cast a little better.

SPOUTERS

These bugs, which aren't nearly as common as poppers or pushers, shoot spouts of water up in the air on the retrieve. They have an irregular face that's hard to describe—a sort of slanted triangle dished out on either side. As the inventor, Bill Gallasch, put it, the face is "sort of half moon shaped from the center of the bug."

I haven't fished extensively with spouters because they aren't commonly available in tackle shops and are difficult to make. But they have caught bass for me, and the action looks good. The significance of the water spouts isn't entirely clear to me, but, hell, it's something different—and that alone might sometimes be enough to do the trick!

SLIDERS

These bugs have pointed or bullet-shaped faces and therefore create less surface ruckus than poppers, pushers, or spouters. They are ideal for fast retrieves in

Slider bugs have a pointed face and bullet-shaped body. (Courtesy Accardo)

lunging or zigzag patterns, and they can also be effective with slow, twitch-and-rest retrieves. If rigged with hook guards, they're very good for fishing in weeds and grass because they don't get snagged as readily as snub-nosed bugs.

DIVERS

Some lures are difficult to classify. The original Rapala balsa plugs, for example, are sometimes classified as crankbaits, but I think they're better classed as topwater baits, although they will dive a little when retrieved. Some bugs work the same way, a good example being the deer-hair Dahlberg Divers, which are discussed in the next chapter.

I've made divers from cork bug bodies simply by reversing slant-faced bugs on the hook so that the cork is upside down. Further, any floating bug can be made to dive by fishing it with a sink-tip line.

PENCIL BUGS

These are long, slender cork or balsa bugs with a fluffy tail. Some have a flat popper face and some are pointed. I like either design in all white and I like to twitch them

Pencil popper (Courtesy Betts)

along on the surface, like a wounded minnow. Several designs have a popper-shaped face and sport tail feathers tied to flare out. These, often tied on 1/0 hooks, are usually painted white or pearl and marketed for anglers after white, striper, and hybrid bass. They will also take black bass.

Sometimes I weight the bend of the hook with a small splitshot or lead wire, adjusting the weight so that the bug sits at 45 degrees in the water. Then I plunk it along, fishing it like a stick plug.

GERBUBBLE BUGS

These cork or balsa bugs are flat on the top and bottom; the sides are grooved or slit to receive a feather, which is glued in place with the fibers sticking straight out. The bug also has a feather tail. I like the Gerbubble Bug design because it looks bigger without adding much extra weight. The principle can also be used with hair bugs.

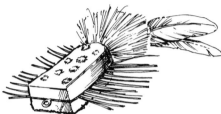

The Gerbubble Bug has a saddle-hackle "leg" inset into a slit in the balsa-wood body.

RUBBER-SKIRTED BUGS

Most of the bass bugs made with cork, balsa, or plastic bodies are dressed with feathers or hair. A few, however, such as the fly-rod version of the Arbogast Hula Poppers, are fitted with rubber skirts. These can be very effective. The secret is in the action of the skirt when the bug is dead in the water. If the skirt is working properly, the strands of rubber will move about on their own, slowly curling outward and upward. The way to take advantage of this enticing movement is to pause 30 seconds between pops or twitches.

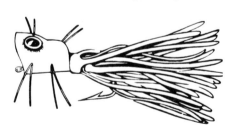

Hula Popper with slip-on rubber skirt (Courtesy Arbogast)

It is important that the rubber skirt be of top quality and in good condition. It must seem alive in the water; a dead skirt just doesn't have that subtle, enticing movement. I suppose that long storage in general is bad for a skirt, but the quickest way to kill one is to store it in a hot place or to overexpose it to sunlight. Also, the paint on some lures apparently reacts chemically with the rubber skirt, causing a half-melted, tangled mess. The best bet is to store skirts (dry) in plastic bags or in a small bottle of distilled water. A pork-rind jar will do nicely.

Slip-on plastic skirts are also available. Although plastic skirts are easier to keep in good shape and work nicely enough on fast-moving lures, I feel that rubber works best for slowly fished surface lures and for any lure used in cold water.

Small rubber skirts can be purchased in some tackle shops, and I often buy them to dress up old bass bugs with unraveling hackle or hair. First, I remove all the hackle or hair with a razor blade. Then I thread the skirt onto the hook and snug it up to the body of the bug. Then, working from the rear, I wedge the skirt tight with trimmed matchsticks or toothpicks. Another method is to trim off some of the old hackle or hair, leaving enough body to wedge the skirt properly. Remember that the skirt can be put on in reverse fashion. This will make a more bushy dressing on the retrieve, but it will also create a good deal more wind resistance on the cast.

Living Rubber, which was originally used for corsets and other items in the garment industry, has been used as bass bug legs for a long time. Hand-tied Living Rubber skirts became popular on jigs and spinnerbaits a few years ago, and the same techniques can be used on bugs. Also, a number of other skirt materials, such as Lure-Fil, are now available for do-it-yourselfers. (Anyone interested in tying skirts and other dressings from these materials may want to take a look at my book *Luremaking: The Art and Science of Spinnerbaits, Buzzbaits, Jigs, and Other Leadheads*, Ragged Mountain Press, 1994.)

RUBBER-LEGGED BUGS

Many bugs on the market have rubber legs, normally three or four on either side of the body. I usually prefer bugs with legs, especially when fishing with bugs small enough to catch large bluegills. Another point: Rubber legs help balance a bug in the water, whereas some bugs without legs tend to turn over on the retrieve, causing the leader to twist. On the other hand, rubber legs add both weight and air resistance to a bug.

Betts Bug with rubber legs (Courtesy Betts)

Rubber legs tend to tear off, mat, or become stiff with age. Much depends on having good rubber hackle to begin with, and then on storing the bugs properly. It is possible to replace rubber legs on cork or balsa bugs by threading them through the body with a needle, but whenever I have problems with legs I merely snip them off flush with the body and then use the bug without legs.

Rubber legs made from "round" rubber, which is simply another form of Living Rubber, are now available. Living Rubber is also available in several diameters, although the regular size is still best for legs on most bass bugs.

Because Living Rubber isn't very durable, the do-it-yourselfer may want to experiment with legs made from some of the newer skirt material, such as Lure-Fil.

HAIR BUGS

Hair from deer, caribou, and elk is hollow, making it ideal for constructing floating bass bugs. For do-it-yourselfers, hair bugs are easy to make. Gobs of hair are "spun" onto a bare hook, which leaves a lot of hair sticking out and the unfinished lure looking like a blob. Then the hair is trimmed down so that the bug resembles a frog, a moth, a mouse, or whatever. In truth, such trimming isn't really necessary, and an untrimmed, bushy bug often can be more effective on largemouth bass, although it may be more difficult to cast than its closely trimmed counterpart.

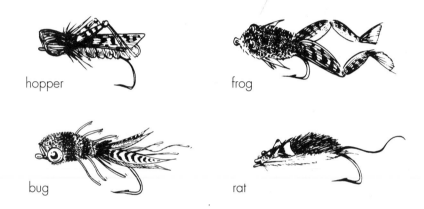

hopper

frog

bug

rat

Bugs and lures tied with deer body hair. (Illustration by Dave Whitlock, courtesy Scientific Anglers)

The main point in favor of hair bugs is that they are lighter than those made of cork or hard plastic. Despite high wind resistance, large hair bugs can be cast relatively easily, and they hit the water a bit more gently than most other bugs, provided that they're dry. (Soggy bugs are much heavier and tend to splash down.) Hair bugs, if well made, also last longer than cork or balsa bugs, and the hair soaks up scents better, too, for those so inclined. Deer hair itself has a natural scent, which may attract bass.

Hair bugs can be fished pretty much the same way as poppers or pushers. Twitch and rest, twitch and rest. Slowly. But be sure to try the frogs and mice on a run-and-rest retrieve; that is, move them by hauling in line, so that the lure runs for 6 inches to a foot, then rests for a few seconds. Also try a slow, steady retrieve with a hair bug, producing a heavy wake in the water. A hair rat fished in this manner can be deadly on largemouth bass. And on gars.

It's possible to alter the action of hair bugs by using fly or line dressing. As Charles Waterman pointed out in the January 1975 issue of *Florida Wildlife:* "If you want them to pop loudly, don't put any dressing on them. If you want the top part to stand up high and the lower part to get a little waterlogged and pop a little, dope the upper section with line dressing. If you want them to stand up and just dance on the surface, dope the whole works." Another tactic that can be deadly is to fish a waterlogged hair bug with a slow, steady retrieve, making the bug swim along almost under the surface. This retrieve will produce a heavy wake.

A semiweedless lure can be devised by trimming the bug so that the point of the hook is flush with the hair body. You may miss some strikes with this rig, but you'll probably get more strikes because you'll be able to fish in lily pads, weeds, and other cover.

MUDDLERS

The original muddler minnow has a deer-hair head, a gold tinsel body, and a wing and short tail of brown turkey over gray squirrel. But muddlers now come in many variations. All have deer-hair heads, and most (some are weighted) can be fished either wet or dry, depending on whether or not the head is dressed with flotant. When fished dry, a muddler creates a buglike ruckus on the surface, and it can be effective when fished with a slow, steady retrieve. I am fond of fishing a sparsely dressed muddler on top for a few twitches or "pops," then letting it sink slowly, twitching it slightly as it goes down. Usually, I fish the muddler all the way to the bottom, then hop it along for several feet.

Don Gapen's original muddler (left) had a clipped deer-hair head and sparse dressing. Many variations have a similar head and a fuller dressing, such as the Bailey Marabou Muddler (right).

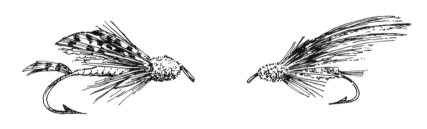

If I had to choose one lure for all my fly fishing, it would surely be a muddler—to be more specific, a black marabou muddler. Muddlers are, in my opinion, the most versatile of all fly-rodding lures.

SPONGE SPIDERS

Small spiders with sponge rubber bodies and rubber legs are terrific for bluegills, and the larger sizes will also catch bass. Sizes 8, 10, and 12 work best for bluegill. Sizes 4 and up work best for bass. Although size 6 will catch either species, it isn't ideal for either one. For bluegills, sponge spiders should be fished very slowly, letting them sit dead in the water for 30 seconds or even longer; for bass, however, they should be fished much faster, in my experience. Foot-long hauls can be effective, but I usually cast them out and fish them on a slow pickup. I hit on this retrieve when winding in my line at the end of a bluegill session, and again when trolling my line behind the boat while I was rolling myself a cigarette!

I seldom tie on a spider for bass—at least not especially for bass. When I'm after bluegills, however, I'll often use a spider for both bluegills and bass. The trick is to fish the spider very slowly for bluegills, then fish for bass with a sliding pickup.

Sponge rubber bug with rubber legs is better for bluegills than for large bass.

MINIATURE PLUGS

One of the best bass catchers available to baitcasting and spinning buffs is a balsa (or plastic) plug that can be twitched about on the surface, then pulled under for a wiggle retrieve. Although a few plugs such as the 2-inch floating Rapala can be used on a fly rod, most plugs on the market are simply too heavy. It is, however, not too terribly difficult to make balsa lures, and some of the better baitcasting plugs, such as the original Big-O, were carved by hand.

One problem with miniature plugs, aside from weight, is that treble hooks—especially the belly treble—tangle frequently in the fly line or leader. Remember that the line and leader form a loop during the cast, and that the fly (or lure) must turn over at the end of the cast. Anyhow, if you want to try any lure with treble hooks, the tangle problem can be held to a minimum by using a hefty fly rod, an appropriate line, and a short, heavy leader. But note that a heavy tippet can kill the action of a balsa plug, so using a tiny split ring in the lure eyelet is advisable.

Although tiny plugs can be used on a fly rod, I feel that they're better suited to ultralight spinning rigs.

DRY FLIES

Smallmouth, redeyes, and other bass can be caught on dry flies, but you'll usually do better (much better) with bugs and other lures. It's a matter of visibility, I think. In addition to their small size, most flies tied for trout sit on the surface film instead of actually in the water. Unless bass are actively feeding on a hatch, they aren't likely to notice such dainty offerings from any distance away, and, of course, dry flies aren't attractors because they don't create the surface ruckus associated with poppers and other bugs. Some writers, however, have other opinions on this matter, and some books on bass fishing or bass flies list even size-12 flies for bass.

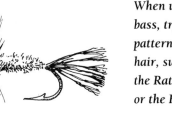

When using dry flies for bass, try large, bushy patterns tied with deer hair, such as the Wulffs, the Rat-Faced McDougal, or the Humpy.

Dry flies can be presented very softly, and this might be an unexplored application for the larger sizes, especially when you're casting to skittish bass in shallow water. Large Wulff patterns, tied rather bushy (check the mail-order catalogs under "salmon flies"), will take bass if they're fished like a bug. And anglers who tie their own flies can experiment with large parachute patterns (unavailable commercially, so far as I know), which sit *in* the water instead of *on* it.

SOFT PLASTIC LURES

All manner of bugs and frogs and things are molded from soft plastic. Some of these lures will float if they're used with small, light hooks. And they will catch lots of bass. I seldom use them myself, however, because they tear too easily or too often twist around on the hook. On the other hand, a bass often will hold these lures quite a while; consequently, a soft plastic frog or something similar might be a good choice for the fly-rodder who forgets to keep a tight line or who fails to keep an eye on his bug!

CHAPTER 6

RUNNING SHALLOW

The ultimate in fly-rodding for bass is the thrill of a lunker striking a topwater bug. But if the bass won't come up, the complete angler must be prepared to go down. Often this is merely a matter of tying on a sinking lure without changing the floating line. If you intend to fish deeper than about 5 feet, however, you should consider a sinking or a sink-tip line.

Most wet flies and streamers on the market are tied for trout and just aren't large enough for bass, unless you're after redeyes and other species that don't average much more than a pound. To be sure, small lures will catch some bass of any sort, but I firmly believe that day in and day out you'll catch more bass with size-2 and larger flies. I prefer streamers at least 4 inches long for largemouth bass, and usually for smallmouth. Larger flies and lures are easier for bass to see, and they make more vibrations, or stronger ones, on the retrieve. I might add that every bass, not just largemouth, has a large mouth for its size, and that bass feed more by hearing than by sight.

But smallmouth and other bass at times prefer small fare, as when the water is colder than normal and their metabolism lower, or when they're intent on a school of small baitfish. So, if you have a bunch of trout flies, don't hesitate to try them in bass waters, especially if you don't mind catching lots of small bass, bluegills, and such.

Trout flies, small streamers, and nymphs can be "enlarged" by attaching some sort of trailer. I prefer thin, narrow pork rind, but you can use strips of plastic and rubber from balloons, torn plastic raincoats, and such material as surveyor's flagging. I suppose trout snobs will ruffle their hackles at the idea of hanging a strip of pork onto a beautiful trout fly, but the bass don't seem to mind. Maybe they think it's an eel or something chasing a fly.

In any case, no fly-rodder after bass should be without a good selection of subsurface lures. Here's my breakdown:

STREAMERS AND BUCKTAILS

Both streamers and bucktails are intended to imitate minnows, whereas wet and dry flies are tied to imitate insects. There are exceptions, and streamerlike lures can be tied in the likeness of eels, leeches, sirens, tadpoles, and so on. Most of the commercially made streamers and bucktails imitate minnows, however, and should be fished as such. The difference between streamers and bucktails is purely a matter of materials: streamers have feather wings, and bucktails are made entirely from hair.

Dan Bailey's Bucktail Streamer

Any of the streamer or bucktail patterns will catch bass. Some of the saltwater patterns I've tried were excellent, and were large enough to interest even lunker largemouths. I especially like large Lefty's Deceivers, which are tied with a bucktail skirt on the head and a long, flowing, saddle-hackle tail. Note, however, that saltwater flies are usually tied on large, heavy hooks, which must be kept very sharp.

My favorite way to work a streamer or bucktail is to alternate short hauls with pauses. But experiment: fast and slow, rhythmic and erratic. Streamers and bucktails are also effective when used with a spinner attachment; the spinner blade imparts a tight wiggle to the wings. (Spinners are discussed under a separate heading.) I feel, however, that too many bass anglers impart too much action to streamers and bucktails.

A streamer or bucktail merely sinking down naturally is sometimes deadly on bass. A muddler minnow or other slow-sinking pattern tied with deer hair can be especially effective. Eels, leeches, and other such long, slender patterns are usually weighted with lead wire, but they can be very effective tied unweighted with a deer-hair head. The Whitlock Water Pup (essentially a muddler head followed by a zonker strip—a long strip of tanned rabbit skin with the fur on) is a very good design for shallow fishing if tied unweighted. Unweighted or lightly weighted versions of the various sculpin and spuddler flies are also very good when fished shallow. Some of the saltwater patterns tied with deer-hair heads can be fished very effectively just under the surface. These include the imitations of finger mullet, Tabory's Snake Fly, and others.

Slow-sinking Eel Bug by Tim England

WET FLIES

All of the larger wet flies will take bass, but they aren't as productive, day in and day out, as streamers and bucktails. Wet flies are shorter and don't have the same action, but they can be effective when used with a spinner and a thin, narrow pork strip. The length of the pork strip isn't critical, but I prefer mine to be about 1½ times the length of the fly. If the pork strip is a thick one, I take a razor blade and make a split-tail out of it.

NYMPHS

Although the complete trout fisherman will probably profit by knowing a hundred different nymphs, I don't think the bass angler should bother to clutter his head with all this information unless he has an interest in entomology or in fly tying.

I don't think most bass are interested in nymphs either, although I once caught a 7-pound bass on a No. 10 Montana nymph while fishing for bluegills. I considered this to be something of a fluke and I thought maybe the fish had sucked the nymph into its mouth while yawning. Or, more likely, it was after a bluegill that was after the nymph.

Nonetheless, large nymphs such as dragonflies and damsels are abundant in many bass waters, and in some may be an important food source. Down here in south Alabama, however, I've never found a nymph in a bass's stomach, although I've found countless frogs, sirens, crayfish, shiners, leeches, eels, snakes, and even squirrels. In New England and other areas, many stream-dwelling smallmouths are caught on nymphs, and some talented fly tyers like Paul Jorgensen have created extremely realistic imitations using materials such as sheet Latex. They even cut and dye little arrow-shaped pieces of Latex to form individual stonefly wing cases. Although some of these nymphs are almost works of art, I really don't think they're all that effective for black bass, except, perhaps, in giving the angler more confidence in his lure (which can be most important because it encourages concentration and keeps one fishing instead of changing flies). I'm certainly no historian of fly tying, but it seems to me a movement started in the mid 1970s toward increasingly realistic imitations, not only of nymphs, but also of other aquatic and terrestrial creatures. This trend has continued to the present time, giving us all manner of lifelike creations, such as McCrabs.

I don't want to make light of these creations. But, since this book is about catching bass, not about fly tying, I'll have to point to a similar development in fishing plugs that started at about the same time as the realistic Latex nymph movement. I'm talking about photo-painted bass plugs. During the mid 1970s we saw all manner of bass plugs painted to look exactly like pumpkinseed and baby crappie and baby trout (these imitated the trout stocked in some California lakes, which unintentionally fattened up the Florida largemouths that were stocked in the same impoundments. Several largemouths over 20 pounds have been taken from these lakes). These realistic casting plugs, pooped up by magazines and TV shows, sold like crazy for a few years. They caught more than their share of bass simply because that's what people were fishing with. Then sales began to fade. Without knowing quite why, most of us who fished with baitcasting gear went back to the old colors popular in the early 1970s. The first Rapala color—silver sides with a black back—is still hard to beat. I'm not sure, but I don't think that bass could see the realistic plugs very well. After all, some of these fish, such as the pumpkinseed and crappie, have these markings as camouflage, do they not? So, why camouflage your lure?

There is no question that nymphs catch bass in cold water. But I think that the operative concept is cold water, not smallmouth versus largemouth. Black bass—all of them—are warm-water species. In cold water, their metabolism slows down. When this happens, they move about less and require less food. In cold lakes, they tend to stay on bottom in the deeper holes, if the oxygen content is right. In streams, they tend to hug bottom in the deeper pools. They seldom feed actively, but will take whatever drifts by their noses, provided it produces vibrations like something alive. (Bass won't hit lifeless corn, gobs of cheese, or cutbait.) Thus, a fly-rodder's nymph, drifting along the bottom, will sometimes catch bass in cold water, perhaps when all else seems to fail. The key here is getting a slow-moving lure very close to the fish.

In my opinion, the best patterns for this kind of bass fishing are not necessarily those that are realistic. In short, I feel that the nymph selected for bass fishing ought to have some action, even on a dead drift. The old Girdle Bug, with rubber legs and rubber feelers sticking out everywhere, will catch more bass than picture-perfect imitations of the various ugly bugs.

Even so, with the possible exception of cold-water environments, I feel that nymphs (unless they are 3 or 4 inches long) are way out in left field as far as bass baits go. The best thing you can do with a Montana nymph in Florida is to use it to catch an 11-inch golden shiner for bait.

In any case, anyone who drifts nymphs along the bottom of a stream, especially in those containing fallen timber and brush, ought to look into the bug-eye concept, set forth in the next chapter. Essentially, this trick permits the fly tyer to construct weighted nymphs and other such lures that drift along the bottom with the hook point riding up instead of down.

SPINNERS

Spinners can be used with any of the streamers, bucktails, and wet flies, as well as with pork rind, plastic lures, and rubber skirts. Hildebrandt and other firms make spinners in all sizes, including some that are small enough for flies. It's best to match the spinner size more or less to the lure. Although I feel that sonic effect and vibration are more important than flash, most anglers think of spinners only in terms of color and reflection.

A few flies are manufactured with a small propeller-type spinner up front. They'll catch bass, especially with a pork trailer. One trick with these is to raise the rod tip sharply as soon as the fly touches down; this buzzes the surface, and may get a bass's attention. After the short spurt on the surface, let the fly sink down, then retrieve it with fast, foot-long hauls. (If you fish it very slowly, you'll have trouble keeping crappie off your line!)

DAHLBERG DIVERS

These flies, named for originator Larry Dahlberg, are floaters that dive underwater when pulled, then float back to the surface. Instead of a diving lip or bill, they have a small, bullet-shaped deer-hair head and a wide, stiff, flaring collar of deer hair; they look a little like a hornless triceratops. Dahlberg Divers are available in a wide range of hook sizes and variations, and work very well for bass. Picking one up from the water for another cast can be difficult, however, for obvious reasons.

SWIMMING FLIES

Best Tackle Company once marketed a swimming bucktail, called the Stanley Streamer, that had a cupped plastic lip fitted into the head. It came in several sizes, and in some beautiful colors. The action of such a streamer is very good, swimming and wiggling like a plug on the retrieve. The objection that I have is that, like the Dahlberg Diver, the Stanley Streamer is rather difficult to get out of the water. This makes the pickup awkward and gets the backcast off to a bad start. It is, however, great for trolling.

The Summer 1983 issue of *Fly Tyer* contained an article by Tim England about making a Banana Bug, which was inspired by the Helin Flatfish plug. It's a banana-shaped deer-hair floater that dives and wiggles on the retrieve much like the Flatfish.

Tim England's
Banana Bug

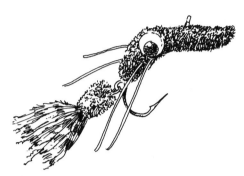

A commercial version of the Banana Bug, with a foam head, is available from Orvis and other fly shops. If you tie your own flies, experiment with various bill lengths—but remember that the hook point should have some bite. A bass usually will engulf the whole lure instead of grabbing the hook end.

Anyone who ties his or her own bugs can come up with a lip or bill made from a strip of thin aluminum or perhaps clear plastic. With experimentation, you can match the action of your favorite plugs with fly-rod lures. For ease of use with a fly rod, such a bug should float to the surface for the pickup. In all honesty, however, it's easier to fish diving plugs with a spinning or baitcasting rig.

SOFT PLASTIC LURES

Worms are by far the most popular and productive bass lures for spinning and baitcasting, and the smaller ones can be used with a fly rod, if somewhat clumsily. In addition to worms, soft plastic lures have been made in the likeness of every sort of critter that bass eat, or might eat. My objection to soft plastic lures is that they are *too* soft and either tear off the hook or don't stay on it straight.

PORK LURES

All the pork-rind baits I've seen will catch lots of bass, either when used with a spinner, or as a trailer, or when merely put on a hook of suitable size. A 2-inch fly strip behind a spinner can be deadly. The 4-inch bass strips, small frogs, and split tails, as well as other pork lures, are great when fished with a small hook, especially around weeds and lily pads. But I'm partial to pork eels, simply because bass, and especially largemouth, feed extensively on eel-like creatures. A 6-inch black eel is in my opinion one of the greatest bass catchers of all time, but it is too heavy for casting with a fly rod. Much of the weight can be removed by cutting off a good part of the belly, leaving a head and the tough, but supple, rind on top.

Bass will usually hold onto pork for some time; consequently, it's best to let the bass "run" a bit before setting the hook. My policy is to lower the rod tip as soon as I feel a bump or pickup, then take up the slack line and set the hook. With short lures, such as pork frogs, I'll strike back immediately.

SPOONS

It's possible to fish tiny spoons with a fly rod, and they will catch bass, with or without a trailer. But most spoons are awfully heavy for their size, whereas the fly-rodder is usually, but not always, looking for large, light lures.

I've made ultralight spoonlike metal lures from the tops of one-pound cans of Sir Walter Raleigh pipe tobacco. Similar lures, designed for bluegills, were described some time ago by John Weiss in a magazine article, to which I owe the idea entirely. Since the article appeared, comparable lures have been put on the market by Fin, but, again, they're designed for bluegills and aren't quite large enough for bass. The lures that Mr. Weiss described are made by cutting a circular piece of light aluminum, folding it over around a slightly undersized hook, and clamping it tight with pliers. The undersized hook is most desirable because it binds the hook's shank in the "spoon." The body of the lure acts like a keel, and the point rides up. The only difference in my bass lures is that I cut them slightly oval in shape so that the finished lure looks more like a shad.

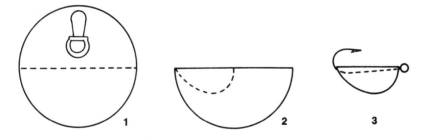

1. Remove light aluminum top from can and fold it in half.
2. Using shears or heavy scissors, cut out spoon body to desired length and shape.
3. Insert hook and clamp sides of spoon tight with pliers. Using a slightly undersized hook will help prevent the body from turning on the hook's shank. Note that the body of the spoon acts like a keel, so that the hook's point rides up.

These lures will catch bass by being cast out and worked back in, as when casting to the edge of a weed bed. They'll flutter down, and can be thought of as slow-fall baits. Be alert for a pickup as the lure drops down, for a bass won't hold these things long. These lures are best suited for casting into schooling bass. Indeed, that's why I started experimenting with them in the first place. Since other lures also can be used for schooling bass, however, I'll discuss the techniques under a new heading.

MATCHING THE SCHOOL

Normally, bass aren't choosy about what they eat. An exception is when bass are feeding on schooling shad and other baitfish. I've seen acres of bass frothing the surface all around frustrated anglers who were casting everything in their tackle boxes without a strike. Apparently the bass are so intent on catching whatever they're feeding on that they just don't see anything else. Although schooling bass sometimes will hit just about anything, the angler will usually do well to match the school not only in color and shape but also in size—exactly.

If you look around in the water, you can usually find a maimed shad on the surface, and chances are good that it will be representative of the whole school of baitfish. You can also find baitfish in the gullet of a bass taken out of the school, but you've got to catch one first.

The retrieve can also be important. The minnows are frantic when bass start tearing into the school, and a fast retrieve works best. In fact, I fish a school by casting out and starting the pickup for the backcast as soon as the lure touches down.

The trouble is that most of the bass caught on the surface of a school will be small. Larger bass sometimes lie suspended under the action, however, and can be caught by letting the lure sink down to them. Bass up to 7 pounds may bunch up tightly when feeding on shad or other baitfish, but larger bass aren't as agile as yearlings, or don't feel as frisky, and don't do as much chasing. (For schooling seasons and related information, see chapter 12.)

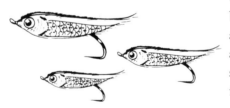

Prismatic minnows for matching the school (Illustration by Dave Whitlock, courtesy Scientific Anglers)

Excellent minnow imitations are available in a variety of sizes. The Whitlock Prismatic Shad, for example, can be tied on long-shank hooks from 8 to 3/0. These have winging made from saddle hackles and a body made from prismatic Mylar tape. Zonkers, which replace feathers with a strip of top-riding rabbit fur, are good minnow imitations when tied with minnow-shaped aluminum bodies covered with braided Mylar tubing. Similar designs use feathers and prismatic material, allowing the complete tyer to imitate shad, alewife, yellow perch, trout, and other good bass food.

DROPPERS

Some fly-rodders are fond of attaching one or more dropper flies to the leader. Special leaders can be purchased with built-in dropper loops, or you can tie a dropper loop or two into the leader. The best bet, however, is to use an extended blood knot. Tie on your leader tippet with a standard blood knot, leaving 6 or 8 inches of extra monofilament sticking out to tie on the dropper fly (clip the other end right at the knot).

Frankly, I think that, in most cases, bass anglers will do well to forget about droppers and concentrate on casting one lure accurately. When you are fishing visible cover and shorelines, accuracy is of utmost importance, and a dropper tied 3 feet from the tail fly won't get in close enough to the cover. Droppers cause tangles, complicate things in general, and just don't pay off in the long run.

The main application of droppers is for casting in open water, especially into schooling bass. The action on schoolers can be fast and furious for a short time, so that the more lures you have in the water, the better your chances of connecting. Occasionally you can hook two bass on one cast.

CHAPTER 7

GOING DOWN

Although the fly rod isn't ideal for general deepwater fishing, it does have one application not easily duplicated with baitcasting or spinning gear. I call it *snaking*. The trick is to use a fast-sinking line, a fairly short leader, and a floating or slow-sinking lure. Deer-hair bugs and muddlers are ideal, but cork, balsa, and plastic bugs also work provided they aren't too buoyant for the line. When a cast is made over submerged brush, creek channels, and other likely bass haunts, the fast-sinking line settles to the bottom and snakes over the structure on the retrieve. The lure follows along behind the line, but slightly higher, thus staying close enough to the structure to interest fish, but not so close that it hangs up a lot. If things go according to plan.

A slow, steady retrieve will work, and so will a start/stop or twitching retrieve. The lure can be worked by stripping in line or by manipulating the rod tip, but remember that, if you have a lot of line out, raising the rod very much or quickly stripping in a lot of line will force the lure downward. How high the lure runs above the line depends on the particular lure, the length of the leader, and the rate of retrieve. If you're interested in this type of fishing, experiment in clear water.

Short leaders are desirable when fishing deep with a fast-sinking line whether you use a floating or a sinking lure. A 10-foot leader between sinking line and floating lure will result in a considerable belly in the line, making it difficult to detect a strike and set the hook. A belly can be caused either by an unweighted fly sinking slower than the line or by a weighted fly sinking faster than the line. The ideal situation is for the fly to sink at the same rate as the line, or just a little slower.

Because of differences in density and diameter, the tip and belly of tapered sinking lines sink at different rates, and this too can create a strike-missing belly between lure and angler. New sinking lines are available that eliminate this problem. (Scientific Anglers calls them Uniform Sink lines; Orvis calls theirs Density-Compensated lines). Here, too, it's essential to use a short leader to eliminate a sagging belly.

If you've got a good fast-sinking line, almost any fly or bug can be used in deep water, but a fly that itself sinks pretty fast works better unless you want to use the sinking-line/floating-lure technique. Consider:

WEIGHTED FLIES

Wet flies, streamers, and bucktails can be weighted with lead wire during the tying process, but they're difficult to find in many retail outlets and most of the old patterns aren't weedless. Some of the newer patterns, such as the weedless eel-worm streamer, work nicely for fishing deep, at least near the bottom, and were developed for that purpose. Zonkers, with their top-riding strip of

rabbit fur, have a very enticing action when worked slowly along in deep water. Some of the mail-order houses and tackle shops market weighted flies and streamers in larger sizes. If you tie your own weighted flies by wrapping lead wire around the hook's shank, remember to coat the lead with lacquer before you apply hair, feathers, or body materials to prevent discoloration.

A number of eel-like patterns have been developed for fishing on bottom. Most of these are tied on weighted hooks. (Illustration by Dave Whitlock, courtesy Scientific Anglers)

Weighted flies work nicely with spinner attachments and pork trailers, and weighted keel flies (see chapter 8) are good choices when you are dredging the bottom or fishing deep in thick structure.

JIGS

Small jigs as light as $\frac{1}{32}$ or even $\frac{1}{64}$ ounce are available and can be cast with a fly rod, but I don't think it's a good idea to try to cast jigs weighing $\frac{1}{8}$ ounce and up, unless you wear a hard hat. Being heavy and offering virtually no wind resistance compared with a large hair bug, they travel at high speed on the cast. I've had them hit the boat almost as hard as a rifle bullet.

Although tiny jigs dressed with marabou and other stuff will certainly catch bass, and can be deadly on trophy smallmouth, I personally prefer to add a long, thin strip of balloon rubber or some such trailer. Often a trailer of this sort is effective on a bare jig head, without dressing. Pork strips are ideal, except that they add even more weight to a lure that is already too heavy.

Jigs will catch bass when fished with a slow, steady retrieve, or when hopped and twitched along. But by far the best bet, in my experience, is to move them up for 2 or 3 feet and let them fall back down. Most of the strikes come while the jig is falling, so be alert. Keep a tight line and watch it carefully. Even a minute twitch can indicate that a bass has taken the lure. Sometimes, a line going slack also indicates a strike. If in doubt, set the hook.

After the first edition of this book came out, I wrote a little volume called *Tying Bugs and Flies for Bass*. I thought it would help more bass anglers get into the hobby of making their own lures, which greatly enhances the sport and, I think, allows you to make a better lure than you can buy. There was nothing much new in the book, except perhaps for a jiglike streamer made with an epoxy head and a long flowing tail, designed for fishing deep like a plastic worm. A sort of delayed review (which came out after the book had gone out of print) in one of the fly-fishing magazines said that the epoxy head was a great idea. The problem with such weighted flies, when used for bass fishing, is that they hang up frequently, especially if they are fished on the bottom.

I don't remember whether I covered monofilament loop weedguards in *Tying Bugs and Flies for Bass* (and I no longer have a copy for reference), but I do know that this device seems to be popular on some of the modern surface bugs and streamers. Almost always, however, the best weedguard designs are on lures with hooks that ride up, whereas the monofilament loop usually rides down. In hardware, the modern buzzbait and spinnerbait designs have top-riding hooks and these are quite weedless. A jig hook also rides up, but jigs tend to roll over and hang; consequently, bass anglers using spinning and baitcasting gear usually have to fish a jig that has a weedguard of some sort. Further, a jig is not a very good hooker because it doesn't have much bite; this is especially true of small jigs, sizes 8, 10, and 12. (I don't want to get too deeply into lure design here, but I have treated the subject at some length in my book *Luremaking*.) In short, a fly or streamer tied onto a jig head for bottom bumping isn't much good because it has scant bite and tends to roll over and hang up.

LEAD EYES

A rather new development (which I didn't recognize until my editor started barking out new stuff for me to include in the second edition) may very well influence the shape of fly-tying books for the next quarter century and may even lead to a better way to rig a plastic worm onto a hook.

I'm talking about lead dumbbell eyes. I used bead-chain eyes in *Tying Bugs and*

Flies for Bass, and, of course, I later took note of the appearance of lead eyes in the fly-tying supply catalogs. Brass eyes are also available, and solid brass beads are available in a number of sizes. The main idea, however, is not in the bug-eye effect. It's a matter of weight distribution. In short, properly tied lead eyes permit a fly tyer to make a bottom-bumping fly (streamer or bucktail) with a top-riding hook point. This fly has much more bite than a jig, and, further, the bug eyes, sticking out on either side, can provide some side-swipe protection for the hook point while at the same time acting as roll bars. From tiny nymphs to large flowing eel-like flies, this design has great potential.

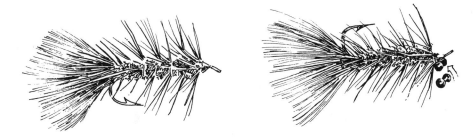

Ordinary Woolly Bugger with hook pointed down. Woolly Bugger tied with lead dumbbell eyes. Hook point rides up.

I hope that the people who manufacture lures will look further into this development, and that layout artists for books and magazine articles and catalogs will realize that it's a matter of weight distribution instead of keying in on the bug-eye effect. But I doubt it. Inevitably, the books, magazines, and catalogs will show the flies upside down in ads and illustrations. After all, they're still printing safety-pin spinnerbaits and doglegged buzzbaits upside down. But we'll see.

PLASTIC AND PORK

All the soft plastic and pork lures are good choices for fishing deep. It's difficult to fish them wrong provided you get them down close to the bass. But this doesn't mean that one retrieve is always as good as another. Day in and day out, the most effective method is to raise the rod tip up over your head, then tight-line the lure back down. Most of the strikes come when the lure is falling, so be ready. Often, a bass will hold onto a soft plastic or pork lure, so that quickness in setting the hook isn't as critical as it is with jigs and other hard lures. Still, you ought to know when you're getting a bite.

There is a practical limit to the depth one can fish by casting. If the structure or whatever you want to fish is 40 feet down and you make a 50-foot cast, your lure will be almost under the boat before it touches down—making your effective retrieve very short. I don't advise casting to structure deeper than 15 feet. At least not with a fly rod, except possibly with a lead-core shooting head and monofilament running line.

The easiest way to fish very deep water with a fly rod is to yo-yo. Or troll.

In yo-yoing, or deepwater doodlesocking, the lure is simply lowered into the water to a suitable depth, then worked up and down. The technique can be very, very effective in submerged timber, and, in fact, it's the only practical way to fish some submerged stands of timber. In one sense, the fly rod, with its long reach, is more suitable than the casting rod for yo-yoing, but the fly reel leaves much to be desired, especially for fishing in very deep water. With either spinning or free-spooling casting reels, the weight of the heavy lure will take it down, whereas with a fly reel you'll have to strip off line by hand. In any case, yo-yoing with a fly rod works best with the heavy lures used with baitcasting or spinning rods, and "jigging" spoons such as the Hopkins are favorites among bass fishermen.

The strike will usually occur when the lure is falling. Set the hook immediately, and set it hard if you're using a large lure with a heavy hook. I might add that yo-yoing in thick stuff requires a heavy tippet—even 15- or 20-pound test.

I once stopped by Lake Ochese in North Florida, near Grand Ridge. It's a natural cypress pond made larger by a dam on the drainage end, resulting in some very thick stands of cypress trees in 30 feet of water. The trees are all in the center of the pond, and there's a good bit of open water between the trees and the bank, which has shoals of grass growing out into the water. My nephew David Livingston was with me, and I was telling him how I'd love to fish the grass with a fly rod. A fellow coming out with a nice stringer overheard me and said that the fish were all in the trees, and that you had to go deep.

I winked at David and grinned at the angler, asking, "Then why have you got those two fly rods in your boat?"

"It's hard to explain," he said.

I knew why. He had underslung spinning reels on his fly rods and had been yo-yoing.

I've never been too fond of trolling for bass even with a spinning or baitcasting rig, and certainly not with a fly rod. If you do want to troll in deep water from time to time, maybe while taking a rest from casting, it's best to use a very fast sinking line, preferably with a lead core. A regular fly line is larger in diameter than a lead-core line, and tends to rise if trolled at any speed.

I prefer weighted flies with spinners and pork attachments for trolling, and I pump my rod quite a bit instead of merely dragging the lure through the water. The floating-lure/sinking-line technique is also effective, but you'll have to troll very slowly. If there's a good breeze blowing in the direction you want to fish, just drift.

Also try soft plastic worms trolled very slowly (or by drifting with the wind), lifting the rod from time to time and letting the worm sink down. Note that if you have too much lead-core line out, a lift of the rod will merely scoot the worm along instead of lifting it substantially.

Remember that about 90 percent of a typical lake or impoundment will be almost entirely bassless, and merely dragging a fly across the lake randomly, without regard to water depth and submerged structure, is pretty much a waste of time. It would be more productive, for example, to troll back and forth over submerged points or islands instead of setting a straight course across the lake. (Likely spots for bass are discussed at some length in Part Three.) And when you catch a bass, drop anchor or throw out a marker immediately so that you can fish the spot thoroughly. When you find one bass, there may be others around. Why troll away from them?

CHAPTER 8

FISHING IN
HEAVY COVER

Most fly-rodders who go after bass like to cast around the edge of weeds, grass, lily pads, and similar cover, but they hesitate to venture a bug into the really thick stuff or hazard a streamer in a partly submerged treetop. The complete bass angler must be prepared to go into the thick of things if there's no action along the edges.

One very good reason for casting on into the grass (or lily pads) instead of merely to the edge of the bed is that during the retrieve the bug or fly will shake the stems underneath the water. Bass can sense this movement, and, thinking it's a frog or something, may well come up to investigate. Weed shaking is especially effective if the bass are actively feeding instead of merely lazing deep in the shade. I believe so strongly in weed shaking that I'll cast into stuff so thick that the bug or fly won't even touch water, but will crawl through the tops like a squirrel. The object is to get the bass's attention and draw it out of the weeds to the open water, but I've had 8-pounders come completely out of the water after lures that hadn't even gotten wet.

One of the most suspense-packed moments in bass fishing occurs when you're working a bug in grass and suddenly see the stems parting a few yards away as a lunker homes in fast. When this happens, I think it's best to keep the lure coming with the same retrieve. If the bass hasn't hit by the time the bug reaches open water, let it rest for a few seconds. If this happens when you're fishing with a streamer or some other sinking lure, let it sink down at the edge of the grass, then make a normal retrieve for a few feet. Next, speed the lure up with a sort of slow pickup as you get ready for the next cast.

Most bass anglers fish a weed bed or similar cover with the aid of a boat and a foot-controlled, bow-mounted electric motor. The technique is to move the boat parallel to the weed bed and out about 30 feet from it. Thus, the angler who makes a 40- or 50-foot cast will be fishing partly in the weeds and partly in open water. I prefer this technique, but sometimes it just won't produce many bass, in which case you shouldn't hesitate to head the boat on into the weeds if the bed is large or wide. A good electric motor will pull a boat through surprisingly thick vegetation if the propeller is protected by a ventilated weedguard. It also helps to get the outboard out of the water, or tilted considerably.

Although a weedguard will cut down on an electric motor's efficiency, it's still a good idea to put one on even if you don't plan to enter vegetation. More than once I've been skirting weed beds and have had to use the electric to move the boat back to a lunker bass that couldn't be worked out into open water. But I hesitate to give anyone advice on what to do when they tie into a real lunker in heavy cover. Personally, I head the boat toward the fish and, at the same time, try to work the fish toward me. You simply can't play a fish under such conditions; if it stitches line through the grass or wraps the line around a couple of thick lily-pad stems, it'll break off. However you decide to handle such a situation, you'll improve your chances of landing a lunker if you use heavy tippets in thick cover. And inspect your leader frequently for wind knots and abrasion. Some types of grass will quickly ruin a monofilament leader. (Also be warned that some pine logs have jagged knots on them as sharp as razor blades.)

One very good way to fish a grass bed is to wade, if the water isn't too deep. Wading gives you a lower profile than if you were in a boat, and this enhances your ability to stalk the fish. But step softly lest bass sense the vibrations. In deeper water, a belly boat gives you the same low profile, and allows very close approaches if you can master the art of silent sculling. Anyone who plans to do much wade-fishing or belly-boating in weeds will do well to cultivate a high backcast, for obvious reasons.

Any nonweedless bug or fly can be used in sparse vegetation if you cast it accurately and coax it along during the retrieve. The trick is to move it gently over lily pads or through patches of grass. One good reason for sticking with nonweedless lures as long as possible is that, strike for strike, they'll hook more bass than weedless lures. But, of course, weedless bugs are necessary in really thick stuff.

Regardless of lure, the direction of the retrieve can be important in avoiding snags in vegetation and in such cover as submerged treetops. Grass stems will often lean in one direction, according to the wind and wave action, and you can avoid some snags by retrieving in the direction of the bend instead of across the stems. In lily pads, it's always wise to maneuver line and lure to avoid those troublesome crotches where the pad joins the stem. In fallen treetops, it's best to retrieve parallel to the limbs instead of across them; further, retrieving a lure from the trunk end toward the tips of the limbs can avoid some severe hang-ups in forks.

There are a few weedless bass flies and bugs on the market, and more are likely to become available as more and more bass anglers discover the joys of the fly rod, and as more and more trout anglers discover the black bass. The do-it-yourselfer can have a ball making the various weedless lures.

MATERIALS AND SHAPE

Deer-hair frogs and mice can be tied so that the body hair covers the hook point. Some other hair patterns, such as the old Henshall bugs, can be tied with a hair "beard" that serves as a weedguard. These hair lures aren't completely weedless, and should therefore be worked very gently when the going gets thick.

Heavy feathers also can be used in the dressing to form a weedguard. At one time, weighted casting flies (Peck's) were very popular for baitcasting, and were available in several patterns. The Silver Doctor and Yellow Sally were favorites. Anyone who ties flies won't have much trouble forming such weedguards if the wings and other dressing are tied upside down. That is, the wings should guard the point of the hook instead of riding high on top. But remember that the weedguard can also keep the hook's point from sticking the fish.

MONOFILAMENT LOOPS

One way to make a bug or streamer weedless is to tie a suitable length of monofilament onto the rear of the hook. Then, after all the dressing has been applied, tie the other end at the head. I don't know who came up with the idea, but it is now used on several commercial bugs and streamers, including hair bugs, various rats, frogs, and eels.

I might add, however, that you shouldn't use any sort of weedguard if you don't need it. One good thing about monofilament weedguards is that they can be snipped off if they aren't needed. The Dahlberg Divers, for example, are usually tied with a mono-filament weedguard. But because they are seldom worked in weeds, in my opinion they don't really need a weedguard.

Hair bug with monofilament weedguard

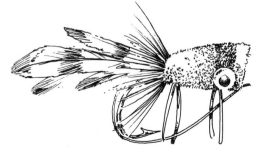

WEEDLESS HOOKS

It's possible to tie streamers and bucktails on weedless worm hooks, which have a wire guard that saddles under the barb, but as far as I know such flies aren't widely available. I have tied some for myself and I like them very much. You can use most any standard streamer or bucktail pattern provided it's big enough to interest bass.

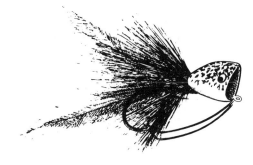

Cork bug with wire weedguard (Courtesy Accardo)

In the past, several commercial bugs were tied on weedless hooks, but these seem to come and go and are often difficult to find in most tackle shops. Arbogast, Weber, and other firms have marketed weedless cork and plastic bugs for fishing in thick stuff.

KEEL HOOKS

Streamers and bucktails can be tied on keel hooks. Because of the weight distribution in the shank, the point of a keel hook rides up, and the wings of the streamer or bucktail act as a weedguard. I feel that flies tied on keel hooks have great potential for bass fishing in vegetation and heavy cover of all sorts. I once fished extensively with a muddlerlike surface lure called Miracle Bug (made by Keel Fly Company) and found that it nosed through grass and brush nicely.

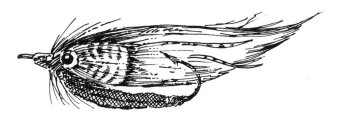

Minnow pattern tied on a keel hook. Note that the hook's point rides up. With some dressings, such as bucktail, the wing acts as a weedguard.

I do, however, have reservations about the hooking power, or "bite," of the keel design. The availability of keel hooks seems to wax and wane with the moon, and several firms have marketed them. One of the best ones I've ever seen for bass was made in England, but it didn't have quite enough bite. Possibly the best bet for the do-it-yourselfer is to get some Aberdeen hooks of suitable size and bend them with needlenose pliers. That way you can adjust the bends to suit your own needs, and you can also drop the point of line-tie down lower so that the hook has more bite. On the other hand, remember that the lure should be bottom-heavy, so that the point rides up. That's the purpose of the keel design.

LIMB HOPPERS

One of my favorite designs for fishing in fallen treetops and brush makes use of hoppers or feelers that don't actually guard the point of the hook. Instead, they jut down on either side of the bug's head and point slightly forward. The idea is to use these feelers to make the bug jump over a limb or other obstruction in the surface of the water. You work the bug right up to the limb, then, upon contact with the feelers, give a short, quick jerk on the line. The bug hops right over the limb—and in so doing might even attract a bass or other frisky fish.

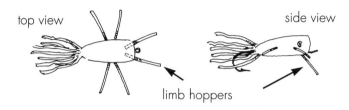

top view   side view

limb hoppers

In the hands of a competent angler, it's a great rig. I don't know who invented the limb hopper, but the first ones I saw were on the desk of Lew Childre, the tacklemaker and father of the Childre Speed Spools, Speed Sticks, and other quality items of bass tackle, some of which are now being marketed by Browning. Knowing that I liked to use a fly rod, Lew gave me a couple of the bugs, which he called *limb hoppers,* and said he'd gotten them from Lefty Kreh. Made of balsa, the bugs had a rather flat body and were sparsely dressed with deer tail. The hoppers or feelers were inserted into slightly slanted holes in the balsa, and were no doubt glued in place. I've made some for my own use with cork as well as balsa, and on one occasion I drilled a couple of holes in a commercial bug and glued in a set of hopper feelers.

The do-it-yourselfer can insert such feelers into cork or balsa bugs and the fly tyer can also work in some mono limb hoppers when spinning deer hair on a hook. Remember that the hopper feelers should be stiff enough to cause the bug to hop over limbs. Remember also that such feelers can cause missed strikes. With this in mind, always point the feelers forward. This forward tilt helps get the monofilament out of the way. In cases where the fish's forward lip does contact the feelers, the forward angle tends to tilt the point of hook right into the flesh.

I have also made cork and balsa bugs weedless by bending a piece of wire leader material into the shape of a hair pin and then sticking the ends through, snugging the U end down tightly, trimming the ends to length, and adjusting the bend the way I wanted it. The monofilament guards are better in some respects, but the design is only semiweedless. The wire design, on the other hand, is much more flexible in that the legs can be bent back over the hook if you want something ultraweedless, or can be bent forward if you want a hopper. I have also seen commercial bugs with V-shaped wire guards on either side of the hook.

Pork eels and frogs, as well as small worms and other soft plastic lures, can be put onto weedless hooks, and, when properly rigged, are the most snag-free of all lures. They're also very productive when fished in weeds and pads because they resemble snakes, leeches, and so on. I often fish such lures rather fast in thick stuff, then let them sink in potholes or at the edge of the weed bed. The idea is to draw the bass out into open water before it takes the lure—but often a fast retrieve brings a strike in the hay. I've had bass hit at such lures three or four times on a single retrieve in very thick lily pads and in grass. Such a fast retrieve can be quite effective at times, usually in the warmer months when snakes and other animals, including bass, are more active. I've even used an automatic reel to zip pork eels along.

But don't rely only on fast retrieves. A slowly worked lure will usually be more effective, and don't hesitate to let a worm or eel lie still for a minute, either on the bottom or atop a lily pad.

Of course, such heavy lures can't be worked in the normal manner with a fly rod. They can, however, be cast out with an underhanded motion, shooting a little line through the guides. This technique is discussed toward the end of chapter 13.

There are a couple of other unorthodox applications of the fly rod for fishing deep in thick weeds, lily pads, submerged timber, and so on. I'm talking about vertical jigging, or doodlesocking. The trick is to lower a heavy lure down into a pothole and jiggle it up and down. The technique has caught tons of bass, and it is really the best way to present a lure to bass in impossible cover. The longer and stiffer the rod, the better it works for doodlesocking. Since no casting is required, spoons, jigs, and other heavy, fast-sinking lures can be used. (Also, a similar technique, which I call yo-yoing, can be used in deep water. See chapter 7.)

I admit that I've done a little doodlesocking when no one was looking and when all else had failed to get a rise, but I can't really recommend using a fly rod in this rude manner, especially when a cane pole will work better. But fly-rodders don't usually tote poles around with them, and it might be a good idea to hide a heavy jig in your fly box, just in case the need arises.

Hell, I've even resorted to jiggerpoling in order to catch a fish. In this outrageous technique, a large floating bug is tied on about 4 inches from the tiptop, then the rod tip is stuck back into inaccessible places. The essential trick here is to shake the rod a little, making the tip splash into the water just ahead of the bug. In other words, the action of the rod tip becomes part of the attraction. Sometimes it's difficult to set the hook because an upward jerk would bang the rod into limbs and brush. A short backward jerk will work if you're quick enough, but, usually, all you can do at the moment of truth is hold on.

Anyone guilty of habitual jiggerpoling with a fine fly rod, I must add, ought to have his name struck from the Orvis mailing list.

M ore than once I've heard that bass are where you find them. True enough. And you'll usually find them in some sort of cover or around some sort of submerged structure. There are exceptions, and plenty of bass have been caught in open water. Nonetheless, you'll greatly improve your chances by keeping your bug, fly, or lure close to visible cover or submerged structure.

"Structure" is a rather broad term that I dislike, but it's now so widely established among bass anglers that it would be foolish to try to communicate by using another term. (The same can be said for "migration route," a term that isn't truly accurate but that communicates nonetheless.) Anyhow, *structure* can be defined as any irregularity in a lake or impoundment bottom, such as a creek channel, a submerged roadbed, or an underwater ledge. The term "substructure" designates an irregularity in the

PART 3

WHEN AND WHERE TO CATCH BASS

structure, such as an island or a high point in a submerged creek channel.

The secret of successful bass fishing boils down to locating the fish and then knowing how to catch them. Knowing something about the ways and habits of black bass will help, but it is equally important to learn the particular lake or impoundment you plan to fish. In theory, the longer you fish a piece of water the more bass you should be able to catch from it, but this doesn't mean that success can't come quickly. Modern bass anglers, with their depthfinders and topographic maps, can learn more about a lake in three days than some anglers would discover in a lifetime. I might add, however, that merely having a fast bassboat fully rigged with all manner of electronic devices won't make an expert bassman out of a poor fisherman, just as a $400 fly rod won't necessarily make an expert bug caster out of anyone who won't slow down long enough to use it.

CHAPTER 9

THE BASSES AND THEIR HABITATS

When I was a boy not much taller than my stack of fishing magazines, I used to read about black bass and wish that we had some in our neck of the woods. We did. We had lots of them. Only we called them trout, or green trout. I had actually caught lots of bass on the local streams and lakes, and no doubt had taken even redeyes and spots. Even today many anglers think only in terms of largemouth and smallmouth, and possibly spotted bass. There are, however, at least 11 species or subspecies of black bass, with much confusion about what's what and where. The host of our local TV show, for example, doesn't know that a spotted bass is a black bass, for he always refers to the largemouth as black bass and spots as spotted bass. He would no doubt be surprised to learn that half the people who watch his show don't know what the term "black bass" means. Maybe it doesn't matter. After he or his guest of the week catches one and shows it on the camera, he'll no doubt catch "anud'en."

The perennial argument over which bass is the better fighter, pound for pound, is in my opinion quite ridiculous. There is far too much difference between individual bass within each species, and far too much depends on where a bass is caught, how it is hooked, how cold or warm the water is, and so on.

There are also some myths along this line. Some anglers believe that a bass caught in cold water will "pull better" and fight harder than a bass from warmer water. This simply isn't true. I've caught bass in water so cold that they hardly pulled at all. (I've also caught bass in water so warm that it made them sluggish.) My experience indicates that bass caught in deep, clear lakes "pull" better than those caught in shallow, murky water, possibly because they're healthier. But this is merely my opinion, and other anglers may well disagree. One thing is certain: any healthy bass caught from a clean stream pulls better than one caught from a lake. As the late Jason Lucas put it, even an old shoe puts up a pretty good fight in current! Another point that's pretty certain is that a bass, regardless of species, caught in shallow water is more likely to jump than one caught in deep water.

I do, however, have a definite opinion on which is the better bass for the *fly-rodder*. It's neither the largemouth nor the smallmouth. It's the little redeye, a relatively unimportant species that I'll discuss later in this chapter. The order of the bass in the following breakdown is based not on my personal preference but on the importance of the species in terms of nationwide availability.

LARGEMOUTH BASS (*MICROPTERUS SALMOIDES*)

The largest of all the black basses, the largemouth bass ranges throughout all the mainland states as well as parts of Southern Canada, Mexico, Cuba, and Central America. It has also been stocked in Africa, Japan, and other places around the globe. The largemouth is by far more adaptable than the other basses and most other gamefish, which makes it a good candidate for stocking. The largemouth's original range included the Mississippi and the Ohio River systems, all the way from the Gulf of Mexico on up into Canada; it extended east to Florida and north up the Atlantic to Maryland.

The Florida largemouth, an important subspecies, can weigh more than 20 pounds. (In the northern states, however, regular largemouth seldom exceed 10 or 12 pounds.) The original range of this bass included only peninsular Florida, southern Georgia, and possibly southeastern Alabama. Recently, however, the Florida largemouth has been stocked in California, Texas, and other states.

As a rule, largemouth show a marked preference for grass beds and other forms of vegetation. They will go deep—and I've caught 8-pounders at 35 feet—but they don't usually go as deep as smallmouth or spotted bass. Because the largemouth is more likely, day in and day out, to hit on or near the surface, I'd have to rate it a tad above the smallmouth as a fly-rod fish. But a lot of anglers, and especially those who fish for smallmouth in streams, will take issue with that statement, and rather hotly so.

As shown in the drawing, the largemouth is easily distinguished from the smallmouth and the other basses because its jaw juts back behind the eye. Also, the largemouth's dorsal fin has more of a gap between the spiny- and soft-ray portions.

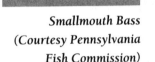

Largemouth Bass
(Courtesy Pennsylvania
Fish Commission)

1. Upper jaw extends beyond eye.
2. Usually has broad black stripe along lateral line.
3. Separation between soft and spiny dorsal fins.

Smallmouth Bass
(Courtesy Pennsylvania
Fish Commission)

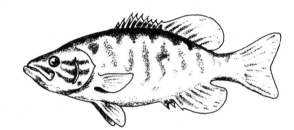

1. Upper jaw does not extend beyond eye.
2. Vertical bars on sides.
3. Not as much separation between soft and spiny dorsal fins.

Largemouth are primarily lake fish, whereas smallmouth are primarily stream fish. It's ironic that the world's record smallmouth (11 pounds 15 ounces) came from TVA's Dale Hollow Lake, and the world's record largemouth (22 pounds 4 ounces) came from a wide spot, known as "Lake Montgomery," in Georgia's Ocmulgee River! Anyhow, largemouth do well in some rivers as well as in some brackish-water areas.

Popping bugs are probably the best fly-rod lures for largemouth, provided the bass are feeding on top. But the largemouth will hit anything that moves in, on, or over the water. Generally, they prefer larger lures than do smallmouth or spotted bass—but I've seen 10-pounders that went for 1-inch lures.

SMALLMOUTH BASS (*MICROPTERUS DOLOMIEUI*)

The smallmouth is easily distinguished from the largemouth because its jaw doesn't jut back past the eye and because its dorsal fin doesn't have as much of a gap between the spiny- and soft-ray portions. The smallmouth doesn't have teeth on its tongue as the spotted bass has, and it doesn't have the reddish eye and fins of the redeye.

The smallmouth's original range was rather restricted, located principally in the Ohio River and Lake Ontario drainage systems. But in the latter 1800s it was transplanted to many states via the railroads. It is still primarily a northern bass, although the world's record breakers have come from Tennessee, Kentucky, and North Alabama. Several attempts have been made to stock the fish in Florida, but with little success. Smallmouth will live in some Florida streams, but will not reproduce in them. The smallmouth has apparently been stocked successfully in some of the colder Texas impoundments. A subspecies, the Neosho smallmouth, grows in the swift waters of the Neosho River and some tributaries of the Arkansas River in the Ozarks. Recent impoundments have pretty much restricted the Neosho's habitat to the upper reaches of tributary streams. The Neosho is a little longer than the regular smallmouth, and can be identified by its lower jaw, which juts out far enough to expose its teeth.

Although the regular smallmouth is primarily a stream fish, it does quite well in cool, clear, rocky impoundments and lakes that are at least 25 feet deep. In general, the smallmouth stays deeper than the largemouth and doesn't feed quite as much on the surface. But bugs and surface lures will catch smallmouth—and lots of them, especially in suitable streams. In either streams or impoundments, smallmouth are fond of rock structure.

Smallmouth seem to prefer smaller lures than do largemouths, which makes them a better choice for those using light fly rods and ultralight spinning rigs. Smallmouth are also more likely to take dry flies, and probably feed more extensively on aquatic and terrestrial insects. I also feel that smallmouth in general feed more extensively on crayfish, but of course a good deal depends on what food is available. They will eat just about anything in the water, and will sometimes gorge themselves, but in general they aren't quite as gluttonous as largemouth.

In impoundments, smallmouth tend to go a little too deep for ideal fly-rodding, but on most days they will move in to the shoreline or to shallow structure early in the morning and late in the afternoon, as well as at night. Early morning and late afternoon are also best on streams, but as a rule a good stream will offer better midday fly-rodding than an impoundment will. Often, the only way to get action on impoundments is to go deep with jigs, jig-and-eel combinations, and similar bottom bumpers.

As a rule, trophy smallmouth are more likely to show up in the impoundments of North Alabama, Tennessee, and Kentucky, but excellent smallmouth fishing can be found from Maine to Oregon, as well as throughout much of Canada.

SPOTTED BASS (MICROPTERUS PUNCTULATUS)

Sometimes called the Kentucky bass, spots seem to be a hybrid between the largemouth and the smallmouth. The distinguishing spots occur in lengthwise rows below the lateral line and are formed by scales that have dark bases. The spotted bass also has teeth on its tongue, which separates it from the smallmouth and largemouth bass, but not necessarily from the Suwannee bass or the Guadalupe bass.

The spotted bass ranges from northwest Florida westward to Texas, Oklahoma, and Kansas, and throughout the Ohio and the Mississippi River systems. In some impoundments, spots outnumber the other basses; in Georgia's Lake Allatoona, for example, from 60 to 80 percent of the black bass caught are spots (but the figures may vary during some years).

There are two subspecies. The Alabama spotted bass grows in the Alabama River system, which extends westward into Mississippi via the Tombigbee River and eastward into Georgia via the Coosa and the Tallapoosa. (They have been stocked in other waters, however, as far away as California.) The other subspecies, the Wichita spotted bass, grows in the streams of the Wichita mountains in Oklahoma.

In most impoundments, spots prefer deep water—up to 100 feet—along steep, rocky banks and bluffs. In my experience, spots in streams also prefer rocky bottom or structure. Because spots are often in deep water, they aren't the ideal fish for fly-rodders, especially in some of the deep, clear impoundments. They can, however, be caught on tiny jigs and similar lures. Spots *will* hit on or near the surface when they're in shallow water, and some streams provide excellent spot fishing for the fly-rodder.

REDEYE BASS (*MICROPTERUS COOSAE*)

Also called shoal bass, Flint River smallmouth, Chipola bass, and no doubt other names, the redeye is a stream fish, and won't normally reproduce in ponds and lakes. It prefers stretches of rocky, fairly swift streams. Compared with largemouth, smallmouth, and even spotted bass, the redeye's range is limited. According to *McClane's New Standard Fishing Encyclopedia*, this species is found in the Alabama, the Coosa, and the Tallapoosa River systems in Alabama; the Chattahoochee and the Flint River systems in Georgia; the Conasauga drainage in southeastern Tennessee; and the Chipola River in Florida. Redeye bass have been transplanted to Texas and possibly other states.

Some confusion exists about what exactly is what, but there seem to be at least two forms of this bass: the Alabama redeye and the Apalachicola River redeye (or Georgia redeye). Generally, the redeye looks like a smallmouth, but can be identified easily by its red eyes; the anal, caudal, and dorsal fins are also red. The Alabama form is usually of a brighter color than the Apalachicola form, but the Apalachicola form usually has a more pronounced basicaudal spot (which may not even be visible on the Alabama form). I've heard, and read, that redeyes grow up to 8 pounds in Georgia's Flint River, but there is some disagreement about these "Flint River smallmouth." Anyhow, the average size of the redeye is about a pound.

The redeye feeds more extensively on insects than the other basses do. In fact, it takes a good part of its food from the surface, and this should be enough to perk up a fly-rodder's interest. Small bugs will usually produce, but the angler should also take along a few streamers and spinners in case the bass are in deeper pools. The redeye puts up a good fight for its size and is noted for its jumping and headshaking tactics. A biologist has called the redeye the brook trout of warm-water species, and I say that pound for pound the redeye has to be the fly-rodder's choice.

GUADALUPE BASS (*MICROPTERUS TRECULI*)

This small bass, which seldom exceeds 12 inches in length, is believed by some experts to be a subspecies of the spotted bass. Others believe it to be a separate species, and *McClane's* treats it as a separate species. Anyhow, the bass is native to the spring-fed streams of Central Texas, such as the Pedernales, Colorado, and Guadalupe rivers. It does live in associated impoundments, but it's primarily a stream fish, preferring swift water in shoals and riffles.

Positive identification is difficult. The Guadalupe closely resembles the spotted bass, but it is a little more spotted. On some specimens the spots occur both above and below the lateral line, whereas on spotted bass they occur only below the lateral line. The Guadalupe has teeth on its tongue (as does the spot), and has 8 to 9 scale rows above the lateral line, 15 to 17 below. (These figures are from *McClane's*; other sources list 7 to 10 above, 14 to 19 below.)

The Guadalupe will take small poppers and other surface lures, but streamers, sparse bucktails, small spoons, and other minnow imitations are probably better. Spinner-streamer combinations are also good.

SUWANNEE BASS (*MICROPTERUS NOTIUS*)

Like the Guadalupe bass, the Suwannee is a separate species that seldom grows longer than 12 inches. This small bass has characteristics of the redeye and the spotted basses. Its distinguishing mark, however, is its bright blue (bluish green, or turquoise) lower belly and chin. The Suwannee's range is limited to the tannic waters of Florida's Suwannee River and its tributaries. I have heard reports of this bass being in the Ochlockonee River in northwest Florida.

One peculiarity of the Suwannee bass is that it usually stays in midstream instead of hanging out around stumps and logs and undercuts in the bank. Also, it seems to feed primarily on crayfish, and therefore doesn't hit surface bugs as readily as the redeye does.

This bass can be taken on any part of the Suwannee River system, all the way to within a mile or so of the Gulf of Mexico. But the best bet is in the swift, rocky stretches of the lower Santa Fe and Ichetuckee tributaries. Remember to fish open water, preferably when the stream is low. A weighted muddler, a Woolly Bugger, or perhaps a deer-hair crayfish pattern may prove successful.

The black bass is considered one of the more intelligent freshwater gamefish in the country. I'm not sure, however, that intelligence is the right word, and anyone who thinks that a bass is smarter than he is will never have enough confidence to make an expert fisherman. I think that too many anglers overrate the intelligence of bass—and underrate their senses.

HEARING

The black bass has an excellent sense of hearing, owing to sensory mechanisms along its lateral line and other parts of its body. It also has an inner ear and a related hollow bone structure that may amplify sound or vibrations. In any case, bass can detect even minute vibrations in the water from some distance away. Moreover, a bass can tell the speed and direction of the source of the vibrations. Thus, the bass can easily home in on a moving lure, or can be alerted to a lure's approach. By the same token, it can easily be spooked by anglers, and is especially wary of such noises as a paddle banging against an aluminum boat, an angler stomping along a bank, or an anchor thrown splashing into the water and thudding down on a rock bottom.

The noise factor is probably more important in quiet, remote ponds and streams than it is on lakes that are heavily fished and constantly used by pleasure boaters. But the large bass in such a lake didn't survive by being insensitive to such blatant, unnatural sounds. In short, the wise angler will avoid all unnecessary noise, no matter where he fishes.

I may be too much of a stickler on this point, but I don't enjoy fishing with most other anglers because they make too much noise in the boat, and are continuously fussing around in their tackle boxes, banging on the bottom of the boat, clanking on this or that. It's true that I'm a bit too fussy. It's also true that I've probably caught more than my share of lunker bass. And I have taken most of them when I was alone and quiet. Sometimes I'll hide behind a tree to fish.

SMELL AND TASTE

Although the bass don't feed as extensively by olfactory senses as a bullhead, it is not entirely insensitive to taste and smell. A good deal of experimentation is currently going on with scented lures, and for some time now plastic-worm buffs have been using this flavor or that. Whether bass are attracted to certain flavors is, in my opinion, open to question. I am, however, certain that some smells and tastes can repel bass, and the fly-rodder will do well to keep gasoline, oil, and the serine in human perspiration off his lures and leaders. I don't think that any sort of added scent is necessary, but I do think you should wash your hands frequently with soap and water and keep your tackle box clean.

One important related point is that many fish and other aquatic creatures emit some sort of chemical substance when wounded. This substance attracts predators, but serves as a warning to others of its kind. Thus, a shiner with a hook stuck in it might attract a bass, but a bass that has been hooked or otherwise hurt can alert other bass in the area to danger. I believe this, and I seldom release a bass in the vicinity in which I caught it. This can be especially important when bass are tightly grouped around deepwater structure, and less important when they're foraging for food along the shoreline. One of the worst things you can do is break a bass off when you're fishing a school. Some of the bass pros are noted for horsing a bass out of the water, and this tactic may be the best way, not because it increases the odds on landing a particular bass, but because it doesn't spook the school as much as "playing" the bass would.

Still another point is that a bass often hits a lure too quickly for its olfactory senses to warn it of danger. But as soon as it gets the lure in its mouth, it tastes the thing and spits it out. The quicker you can set the hook, the better; and the angler who is always alert and expecting a strike will almost always catch more bass than one who doesn't watch his business. I believe this strongly, and I would estimate that when the average angler is fishing subsurface lures that are jigged or allowed to fall in one way or another he will detect less than half of his strikes or pickups.

In recent years, more and more anglers have been using various kinds of sprays and soaks to attract bass and other fish to their lures. Deer hair and feathers can be saturated with liquid to which various scents have been added. But feathers and hair have a natural odor that may be as attractive to bass as packaged scents.

VISION

I've said more than once, both in conversation and in print, that some of the bassboats with high seats mounted on a fishing deck are not desirable for fishing in clear, shallow water. The bass can see you. On the other hand, I've caught bass which, I'm convinced, went ahead and hit because the lure was traveling toward the boat. In other words, the bass hit in a now-or-never situation. I've even caught 7- or 8-pound bass within a few feet of the boat. But I feel that I've lost a good deal more fish than I've caught because of the presence of the boat. I've seen hundreds of bass run at a lure, see the boat, and swirl off. Or so it seemed. In any case, I firmly believe that if you're fly-rodding in shallow water from a high pedestal seat or standing up to cast, you'll do well to make longer casts. You should also avoid white or bright shirts and hats when fishing in shallow, clear water, but I must add that this is my own opinion and that some experts disagree. It's not unusual for professional tournament fishermen, eager to promote a clean-cut image for advertising purposes, to wear such bright clothing while fishing for big money.

I don't believe that bass are quite as leader shy as wild trout, but there is no doubt that a light leader will often produce more strikes. (For one thing, a light leader isn't as stiff as a heavy one, and thereby permits better lure action.) Further, I think that some bass have sharper vision than others. The Florida largemouth, used to chasing frogs and snakes and large shiners, probably doesn't have as keen an eye as does the redeye bass, which feeds primarily on floating insects. I've seen the water literally covered with mayflies or love bugs without a single largemouth rising to them, although they were taking plastic worms fished 4 or 5 feet deep. I don't think the largemouth even saw the mayflies or love bugs, whereas redeye or smallmouth might have been frothing the water after them. Further, I believe that the smallmouth and the redeye are more leader shy than largemouth are. It could be, however, that the largemouth saw the mayflies and just didn't give a damn about them, and that they see heavy tippets and just don't give a damn about them, either! As Charles Waterman said in another context, only the fish know for sure how they see a leader, and they may well disagree among themselves.

TEMPER

Many anglers claim that the bass will sometimes hit a lure not because it wants to eat the thing but because it's angry at it, or just plain aggressive. I too believe this.

There are two approaches to making a bass mad. One is to cast repeatedly to a likely spot with a loud, fast, or outlandish lure. The other is to "play" a bug or surface plug, letting it sit dead for several seconds (or even minutes), then twitching it ever so gently, popping it, letting it sit still again, and so on, much like teasing a kitten with a string. Sometimes the bass will pounce on the lure just to make it move again.

Whatever triggers a bass's temper, I suspect that it is cocked by a territorial imperative, which is, of course, at its strongest when the bass is bedding or fanning out a bed. At this time, a bass will hit a lure just to chase it away from the bed. Other fish will also do this, and I heard of a lowly bowfin (grindle, mudfish, or whatever you call it) that jumped up on a bank after a couple of kids who were poking into a school of newly hatched bowfin fry!

A bass will also take a stand in a pocket or on the shady side of a stump and lie waiting for food to come by. Such a bass can be caught, I believe, on a lure that hasn't necessarily fooled the bass into thinking it's edible. What would you do, if you were a hungry bass and had taken a stand at a strategic spot while waiting for a siren or shiner to come by, when suddenly a popping bug started making enough ruckus on the surface to scare any sensible shiner or siren away? You'd probably sit there for a while, gritting your teeth and cursing the thing. If it kept coming back, you might pack up and leave. Or you might bow up, your gills working faster and faster, until finally you struck the thing.

In all honesty, however, I'm not at all certain that a bass will hit out of anger or frustration except when it's on the bed. Still, I'm convinced that you'll do well to believe this theory. To believe, in other words, that you can catch bass when they aren't biting. Such a philosophy will make you fish harder, and will make your fishing more of a challenge—a personal thing between person and bass.

In any case, it's a known fact that bass, and often lunkers, will hit a lure not on the first or second cast, but on the fifth or sixth. One day, for example, I was experimenting with a fly rod in my boat basin. I must have made a hundred casts near some grass just across the canal, when suddenly a 5-pounder hit my bug violently and came on out of the water shaking its head. The thing took me by such surprise that I didn't hook it, and probably didn't attempt to set the hook. Hell, I wasn't even fishing.

CHAPTER 10

SEASONAL AND DAILY VARIABLES

With such a vast difference in seasonal changes and bass fishing from North to South and from coast to coast—and often within a single state—any irrefutable discussion of fishing by seasons would have to be either quite general or tediously long. As an extreme example, fly-rodding for bass in Florida's Lake Okeechobee can be very good in February, whereas fly-rodding on some of the bass lakes in, say, Michigan, may be impossible unless you're willing to fish through holes in the ice.

If you're unfamiliar with a lake, impoundment, or area you plan to fish, it's best to make inquiries at local tackle shops and marinas, or talk to expert bass anglers and professional guides, before you start fishing. Yet even experts may have false notions about seasonal fishing in any one area, so that local advice may not always be the best. More than one bass angler from out-of-state has shown the local boys a thing or two during tournaments. I fear that many opinions on seasonal bass fishing are based more on the habits and creature comforts of anglers than on those of bass. The new crop of scientific bass anglers, outfitted with a fast boat, depthfinders, and a bionic arm (together with intense concentration and much patience) have proved time and again that bass can be caught winter, spring, summer, and fall, at dawn, noonday, sundown, and night.

Because a good deal depends on geographic location and on the characteristics of a particular lake or impoundment or stream, I believe that such factors as water depth, oxygen content, subsurface temperature, structure availability, and so on are the proper guides to fishing a particular lake at a particular time. These will be discussed later in this chapter. Meanwhile, a few comments on seasonal trends won't, I hope, be too far amiss.

WINTER

Bass tend to go deep when the water gets cold, and they don't feed as much in shallow water even early and late during the day, or at night. The reason they go deep and stay deep is, in my opinion, that frogs, snakes, spring lizards, and so forth hibernate and there simply isn't as much food stirring about along the shoreline or in shallow-water areas. Sometimes, however, you can have a field day by fishing in very shallow water on warm, sunny winter days.

One point to remember when fishing in cold water is that the bass themselves slow down. They eat less, and won't move fast or far to catch a lure. Small baits and slow, deep retrieves are in order.

SUMMER

The so-called summer slump is a myth. Early mornings and late afternoons during the summer are among the most productive times to fish popping bugs. During midday, however, bass are likely to go deep or hole up in heavy cover. Night fishing with surface lures is good in summer months, especially in lakes used heavily by pleasure boaters.

FALL

In most areas, fall offers excellent surface fishing. Bass often go on a shoreline feeding binge just before frogs and snakes and such things start to hibernate.

SPRING

Everybody wants to go fishing on a fine spring day, and the bass too seem fond of getting out of their winter holes to roam about. In spring, you can often get good action all day on popping bugs and other surface lures.

SPAWNING SEASON

Spawning season varies from winter to spring to summer. In Florida, I've seen bass bed as early as December. In the northern states, spawning is usually as late as June or even July. In my cypress pond, which is loaded with crayfish, sirens, minnows, and dragonfly nymphs, the bass spawn off and on all year, but mostly in the spring.

More lunker bass are caught during spawning season than in the rest of the year. This is especially true of lunker largemouth, which bed in very shallow water (1 to 5 feet) and often very close to shore. There are several reasons why very large bass are so vulnerable at this time: (1) Old sow bass mill around in shallow water before selecting a bedding spot. (2) They feed heavily just before and just after spawning. (3) Bass will often attack anything that comes near their bed. (4) The angler can spot the beds, which are often 3 or 4 feet in diameter, and can therefore fish to the bass. I have mixed feelings about it, but I have caught some real lunkers by spotting beds. One day, for example, I was fishing with a high school boy who was visiting us at our place on Florida's Lake Weir. He had a new spinning rig and wanted to catch himself a trophy. We caught a few small ones and were fishing along when, thanks to my polarized sunglasses, I saw a faint white circle on the bottom in some 5 feet of water. It seemed to have a shadow on it. The shadow moved off. Quickly I touched the foot-controlled electric motor and backed away. I told the young fellow that there was a lunker bass down there and that he could catch it if he tried hard enough. I quit fishing to coach him. About an hour later, he did hook the bass and wrestled her out. She weighed a little over 11½ pounds! When we got back to the house, everybody wanted to know what I had caught.

As I said, though, I have mixed feelings about catching bass off the bed, and I seldom deliberately go out looking for beds. Smallmouth and other species, as well as the northern largemouth, however, aren't quite as vulnerable as Florida largemouth because they usually bed in deeper water. Smallmouth in some impoundments bed as deep as 20 feet.

SCHOOLING TIME

Generally, bass school more in the summer months, but on some lakes they school in spring and fall as well as summer. In Florida, I've seen minor schooling activity in November and December.

So much for seasonal variations. On a daily basis, bass tend to stay in deepwater haunts during midday. Early in the morning and late in the afternoon, as well as at night, they are likely to feed in shallow water. Moreover, they will move from deep water to shallow, and back again, along established paths, such as submerged ditches and creek beds. When they're holding in deep water, they're likely to bunch up pretty tightly. But when they reach a shoreline or other feeding area, they'll usually scatter. They will sometimes seem to school when feeding on baitfish, but bass are individuals and don't follow the mass mentality of, say, schools of mullet. They don't necessarily migrate from one spot to another in a pack, and there will usually be some holdover bass in feeding areas at any time of day. There will also usually be some bass in deep haunts even during prime feeding time.

The bass pros talk a lot about establishing a pattern. It makes sense, but remember that there may be several effective patterns for the day. In one tournament, for example, one successful contestant caught his bass in 30 feet of water. Another caught his in 3 feet. So there you have it. Bass are where you find them. Before you start making random casts, however, remember that bass show marked preferences for cover and structure, as discussed in chapters 11 and 12. There are also a number of physical variables to consider.

OXYGEN

The amount of oxygen dissolved in the water can be extremely important in bass fishing. In some cases, there won't be enough oxygen to support them. This usually happens during the hot summer months on the larger lakes, owing to thermal stratification. But decaying vegetation, which consumes oxygen, can also deplete certain areas—or whole lakes.

For most fly-rodding situations in shallow water, there'll usually be enough oxygen to support bass. Even so, the action will be better in areas where the oxygen content is high. You don't need an oxygen monitor to catch fish, but remember that wave action will certainly help oxygenate the water and the spots where waves are breaking on rocky banks or riprap may be hot for a while. Remember also that live vegetation produces oxygen during the daylight hours through photosynthesis.

LIGHT INTENSITY

Because bass have fixed pupils and no eyelids, they have no way of regulating the amount of light that reaches the retina, except by going deeper into the water or seeking out shade. They can and do tolerate bright light at times, especially when they're bedding in shallow water, but generally larger bass do seem to avoid brightness. Whether or not they're actually uncomfortable (and if so, to what degree) in bright light hasn't been settled to my satisfaction. My question is whether they avoid bright light because of discomfort or because they may feel safer or more secure in darker waters.

Whatever the reasons, I do feel that light intensity is very important in bass fishing. Here are some variables that have an influence on underwater light intensity.

Position of the sun. Early and late during the day, the sun's rays hit the water at a narrow angle; reflection is at a maximum, and depth of penetration is at a minimum. Reduced sunlight penetration is the reason why bass fishing in shallow water is usually better early and late during the day.

At noon, the sun's rays hit the water at a 90-degree angle (more or less, depending on the season and geographic location). Reflection is at a minimum, and depth of penetration is at a maximum. This is why shallow-water fishing is generally poor when the sun is high, unless heavy cloud cover is blocking out the sun's rays.

Graph of light penetration when the sun's rays strike the water's surface at different angles. Data taken on a clear-water lake on a bright day.

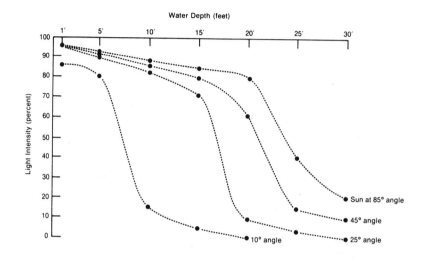

Using a Depth-o-Lite meter on a very clear lake, I once made a series of light intensity readings at various depths during selected times of day. The curves shown in the accompanying graph are based on these readings. Notice that there is a sharp drop in all the curves, and that the drop occurs quite deep during most of the day. This sharp drop represents a sort of twilight zone, and this is where the larger bass are more likely to be. At least in theory. When they aren't spawning.

Depth of water. As the graph shows, there are definite relationships between depth of the water, angle of the sun, and light intensity. Since bass can't regulate the amount of light hitting the retina of the eye, it stands to reason that they will simply go deeper to avoid bright light. This is generally the case with larger bass, but there are exceptions. On the clear lake where the readings were taken, I've caught lunker bass at high noon in 5 feet of open water during July, when, according to the theory, they should have been 30 feet down.

Shade and cover. Anything in the water or on the bank that provides shade will of course reduce the underwater light intensity. Shade might be provided by such vegetation as lily pads, by stumps, logs, and timber, or by high bluffs.

The bass angler will usually do better to fish the shady side of a stream, lake, stump, or dock. Often the shade of a thick tree, such as a cedar, will provide the key to locating bass in other cover or structure. Early or late during the day, the shadow of such a tree will extend far out into the lake or stream, and cover, such as stumps, in this shaded area may be worth concentrating on.

Cloud cover. The position of the sun isn't as important on cloudy, overcast days as it is on bright days, and some of the best bass fishing I've ever had was in shallow water on overcast, misty days. The accompanying graph shows the underwater illumination at 10 A.M. on a sunny day and at 10 A.M. on a cloudy day. These readings were made on a clear lake; they would be lower in murky water.

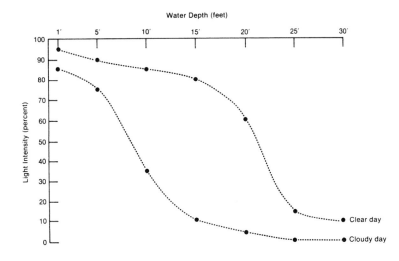

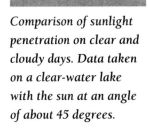

Comparison of sunlight penetration on clear and cloudy days. Data taken on a clear-water lake with the sun at an angle of about 45 degrees.

Wave action. All waves—from gentle ripples to whitecaps—have a bearing on underwater light intensity. During midday, waves tend to impede light ray penetration. Waves cause more refraction and reflection than would occur on a smooth surface. In late afternoon and early morning, however, wave action may cause more underwater illumination than would occur with a smooth surface. When the sun's rays hit at a narrow angle, they tend to reflect. A choppy surface may "catch" some of these rays and direct them downward.

Other aspects of wave action are discussed later in this chapter.

Water clarity. I believe that bass living in a gin-clear lake are more accustomed to high light intensity than bass living in a murky lake, just as someone who works in the out-of-doors is more accustomed to bright daylight than someone who works in a dimly lighted warehouse. For this reason, I don't believe that the ideal light intensity for bass is a fixed value. I suggest that it may well vary from one body of water to another.

In any case, a change in water clarity will often have an effect on bass and their daily habits. Bass will be in shallow water more than usual when a normally clear lake suddenly becomes stained for one reason or another. Topwater lures are often very effective at such times. And the angler should never fail to fish the area where clear water mingles with murky. This interface can sometimes provide fantastic fly-rodding.

TEMPERATURE

When I was fishing with one of the bass pros, I asked him how much importance he placed on water temperature. None whatsoever, he replied. This is a far cry from the advice many of the experts were handing out a few years ago. Shortly after the electronic temperature meters came on the market, a lot of bass anglers—including this one—were spending a lot of time probing the depths for the ideal temperature.

To be sure, I still feel that water temperature is important and has a bearing on how one should fish, but I really don't think it's a reliable indication of where bass will be or won't be. Bass are cold-blooded creatures and probably don't give a damn about temperature, within reasonable limits. In short, I think that dissolved oxygen content, food availability, light intensity, and other variables, together with normal daily and seasonal habits, are far more important than a few degrees of temperature one way or the other. I've caught too many bass in water from 40 to 85 degrees to put much stock in temperature as an indicator of where to find bass.

On the other hand, temperature does affect a bass's metabolic rate and eating habits. Generally, bass in cold water eat less and don't forage about as much, and most knowledgeable bass anglers tend to use small, slowly fished lures in cold water. Bass do apparently become sluggish in very warm water, but, as I said, I've caught bass in water up to 85 degrees. (Geographical location might have a lot to do with the upper limit.)

Whenever you do find bass in the ideal temperature range, they'll probably be easier to catch, simply because their metabolism will be at its highest. This temperature range is generally believed to be from 65 to 75 degrees for largemouth bass, 60 to 70 degrees for spots and smallmouth. But I think this ideal range may shift considerably in some lakes. After all, there is a considerable difference in mean temperatures from Mexico to Canada. And if the bass in some of the small, shallow South Florida lakes didn't eat until the temperature dropped into the ideal range, they'd starve to death. I might add that in one day I've caught about a hundred bass from such a lake when the temperature was above the ideal range.

BAROMETRIC PRESSURE AND WEATHER CHANGES

Compared with the changes in pressure a bass experiences when it moves only a few feet up or down, changes in barometric pressure are downright infinitesimal. It's my opinion that barometric pressure per se has no influence whatever on bass, on how well they bite or don't bite. On the other hand, cloudy weather associated with rapid changes in barometric pressure can cause bass to feed shallow, and some phenomenal catches of bass have been made when hurricanes were moving in.

If I had to draw any conclusions based on my personal experience together with the opinions of others, I would say: Fish deep during high pressure and shallow during low. But take this with a grain or two of salt.

WIND

A warm, sunny afternoon and a calm lake make for good casting conditions, but fishing is often better when there is some wind and wave action. This is especially true in shallow, clear water. Although I'm fond of fishing a mirrorlike lake early in the morning and late in the afternoon, I've caught lots of bass—on surface bugs— when the waves were reaching whitecap proportions. It's difficult to fish in such weather, but a bassboat rigged with a bow-mounted electric motor and convenient push-button electric-winch anchors makes it easier, provided that you learn to cast a bug in windy weather.

There are several reasons why wave action helps the angler: (1) A ripple on the surface makes it more difficult for bass to see you, which can be important in shallow water. (2) Wave action helps oxygenate the water. (3) Waves wash insects and other food across the lake; this attracts bluegills and baitfish, which in turn attract the bass. (4) Wave action gives a surface lure motion and activates hackles and rubber legs on bass bugs. (5) As mentioned earlier in this chapter, ripples on the water can reduce underwater light intensity.

LUNAR POSITIONS AND THE SOLUNAR THEORY

I haven't changed my thinking on such matters since I published, some years ago, the following comments in my book *Fishing for Bass*:

Fishing columns in many newspapers, as well as in some of the outdoor magazines, publish daily, weekly, or monthly Solunar Tables. Worked out over three decades ago by John Alden Knight, the tables are based on the changing position of the sun and moon in relation to the earth.

The Solunar Tables show the time of day when feeding activity is likely to be at its peak. Each daily listing includes a major and a minor period for a particular longitude, and the periods for the immediate future can be calculated by adding about 50 minutes per day. If, for example, a minor period is listed for 1:00 P.M. on Monday, the minor will be at 1:50 P.M. on Tuesday and at 2:40 P.M. on Wednesday. A major period lasts from 2 to 3½ hours; a minor, from three-quarters of an hour to 1½ hours. Although the minor is shorter, bass may sometimes feed more actively than during the major.

Some anglers fish religiously by the major and minor periods, but I personally don't put that much faith in them. I've caught too many lunker bass at times when neither the major nor the minor periods were in effect, and I've too often been skunked during major and minor periods. I do, however, believe that anglers have a better chance of catching bass during a major or minor. But I don't think they should stay off the lake merely because a major or minor isn't in effect. I'm certain that those people who swear by the tables will indeed catch more bass during a major or minor, but I suggest that they probably fish harder and with more confidence during those periods. It is, in my opinion, an error for the bassman to explain success or failure by whether or not the fish are biting. The better philosophy is that the bass will bite at any time of the day or night if the angler can locate them and present the right lure in the right way.

There is no doubt something to the tables, and many anglers can plan their fishing trips accordingly. Believers with enough leisure to choose when they fish should purchase a copy of *Moon Up-Moon Down*, by John Alden Knight . . . .

Apart from the Solunar Tables, some anglers fish by the phases of the moon or by "signs" on calendars and almanacs. Many say, for example, that fishing is best three days before and three days after a full moon. I don't say that these people are loony, but again I don't believe a person ought to stay at home because the moon is full or isn't full.

WATER FLOW

Most anglers don't realize it, but water flow can be extremely important when fishing some impoundments. If the turbines and gates are shut off, there may be little or no flow. But if the turbines are operating or the gates are open, or both, water will flow to some degree throughout the impoundment; and there will be more flow in the river and creek channels. In coastal regions, brackish-water bass tend to hit best on a rising tide, and the water flow no doubt has something to do with this. I don't know exactly why flow should be so important, but I submit the following thoughts on the matter:

1. A flow washes bits of food about, which in turn makes crayfish, minnows, and so forth more active.
2. The bass in most impoundments are from the original stream or river, so that a flow is a natural condition for them; static water is unnatural.
3. A flow may help oxygenate the water, or, rather, cause more water (and therefore more oxygen) to pass over the bass's gills. I talked with one expert smallmouth angler who seemed to think that bass get sort of hyped up during major flow periods.

For whatever reason, bass will sometimes quit biting when the flow is stopped. I mean totally quit.

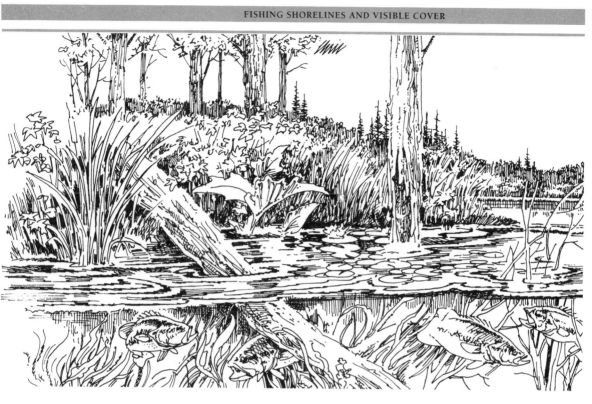

CHAPTER 11

FISHING SHORELINES AND VISIBLE COVER

At one time, just about all bass fishing took place along the shoreline. Then deepwater-structure fishing came into vogue, and a lot of bass anglers, armed with depthfinders and temperature probes and other new gadgets, started looking for hot spots all over the lake. They found them. A lot of pluggers of the old school felt left out; not having anything to cast toward, they simply didn't like to fish in open water and were reluctant about plugging the shoreline and grass beds because they felt they were missing the real action. The fact is that the expert bass angler can do very well indeed by casting to visible cover. John Powell and other bass pros have proved this, time after time, by winning major bass tournaments in shallow water. After all, bass come to the shoreline to feed, and a feeding bass can be caught.

I feel that the fly-rodder will also do well to specialize in shallow water. It's really more fun—and sometimes a fly-rodder can outfish hardware slingers because of the importance in shallow water of a gentle lure presentation. In any case, here are some likely spots to try.

STUMPS

Any stump sticking out of the water near a shoreline is enough to perk a bass angler's interest. Individual stumps aren't likely to hold a group of bass at any one time, but a good stump can pay off over the years. As soon as a bass is caught from around a good stump, another one is likely to move in. Of course, one stump might not be as good as another, and remember that visible stumps in a heavily fished lake, impoundment, or stream are fished by every angler that comes along. Some of the most productive stumps are those that are normally submerged, and marking these carefully during low-water periods will surely pay off during subsequent fishing trips.

Stump field

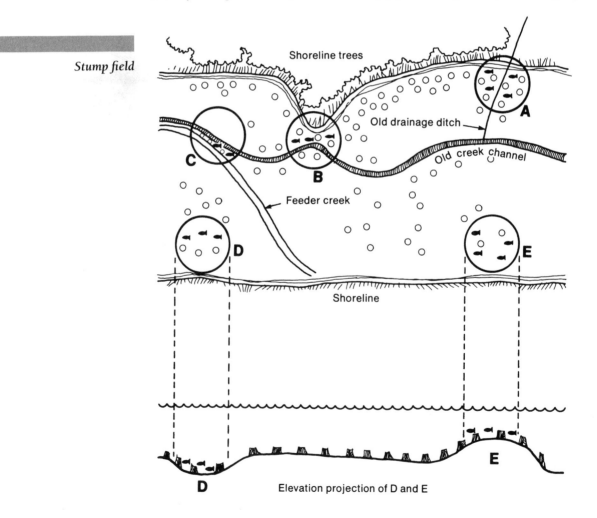

Elevation projection of D and E

Stump fields in impoundments, made by cutting timber before the land was flooded, are another matter. For one reason or another, individual stumps in such fields may be better than others, and also, one stump field, or section of a field, may not be as good as another. Take a look at the accompanying diagram. Assume that the stumps are in shallow water, and then consider related structure. While it's true that all the stumps might hold bass, you'll increase your chances by concentrating on points A, B, C, D, and E.

The drainage ditch or draw from the river channel to A could serve as an excellent migration route; this, in turn, could mean that the stumps around A might provide excellent fishing when the bass are feeding. The point at B might also be a good spot, especially since the point is near a bend in the creek. Stumps at C, which might well be submerged, could be very good; the point where two stream beds meet is always worth investigating.

Depth variations can also cause bass to gather at a certain cluster of stumps, as shown at D and E. Generally, the fly-rodder will be more interested in E—and often the bass will be, too.

One other point. When fishing in shallow water, remember that stumps can provide a little spot of shade, like an umbrella on a beach. These can concentrate the bass for you, and help pinpoint your cast. You don't necessarily have to move to the "shady side of the lake" in order to fish in the shadows.

LOGS AND TREETOPS

Individual logs and trees, as distinguished from submerged stands of timber, that have fallen into the water along the bank often provide excellent bass hangouts, especially in natural lakes and streams. They are sometimes good in impoundments, but flooded timber in many impoundments rather distracts from the importance of a single tree or log.

When fishing a log, remember that the bass will usually be either under it or lying on the shady side of it. Choose your casts accordingly, and try to avoid hooking the bass on the far side of the log. Retrieving a lure parallel to the log may pay off, but remember that the bass will usually be looking out toward open water instead of facing the bank. Therefore, if you're fishing from a boat and cast parallel to the log and toward the bank, you'll throw the bug behind the fish, and might well spook it. Usually, it's best to cast short of the mark, fish the lure a few feet, pick up and cast a little farther, and so on until you've fished the length of the log. If the log submerges, try to project it mentally and fish it out accordingly.

Fallen treetops are often better than bare logs, but they're more difficult to fish thoroughly. As was pointed out in chapter 8, it's best to cast toward the base of the tree, or toward the base of any particular limb, in order to avoid hanging the lure. Also consider what can happen when you hook a lunker bass in a treetop. If you cast perpendicular to the trunk of the tree, a hooked bass can easily get under something. If you cast toward the top of the tree, the bass can dive and catch the line in a fork. But if you cast toward the base of the trunk or limb, you'll have a much better chance of working the bass out. Also, it's best to make your first casts around the outer perimeter of the limbs, then work on back toward the trunk.

GRASS BEDS AND LILY PADS

Weeds, grass beds, and lily pads provide cover and shade for bass when they're in shallow water. Often such vegetation is the only sort of cover available in natural lakes. One way to fish it is to move rather fast until you locate the fish, then slow down. It's usually best, however, to concentrate on cover near deep water or near a migration route, if available.

After selecting a likely patch of pads or a grass bed, pay attention to irregularities such as pockets, potholes, and points. Quite often a productive spot is where two kinds of cover meet. I've had good luck where grass meets lily pads, and where boat lanes have been cut through such cover.

Often, a weed bed along a shoreline will have an outside and an inside edge. As a general rule, larger bass will be near the outside. But there are enough exceptions to disprove this rule, especially very early and very late during the day, at night, and during the spawning season.

I always thoroughly fish a small patch of vegetation set apart from the main bunch, except when the sun is high, and this has paid off for me nicely. Over a period of four years, I caught at least a dozen bass from a little clump of lily pads no larger than a coffee table. The patch grew between my favorite grass bank and the boat landing, and I ran past it a hundred times before I saw another angler catch a bass there. I've also had good fishing around a small patch of grass isolated from the main bed.

A major tournament angler and TV bass personality once said, in print, that lily pads are very poor cover, and that bass won't hang out in pads if any other cover is available. This hasn't been my experience. I've seen some patches of pads that were very, very good at certain times of the year. But I've also seen acres of pads that weren't worth a damn.

Still another type of cover you'll sometimes run across is grass or moss that grows on the bottom but doesn't reach the surface. Poppers and streamers will sometimes produce when fished over such cover, but I prefer to use a spinner attachment, not so much because of the flash but because I believe the sonic vibration may rouse a bass from holes in the vegetation.

Lures and tactics for fishing in vegetation were discussed in chapter 8.

BRUSH AND STICKUPS

Any sort of brush in shallow water may hold bass, but you'll do well to concentrate on bushes and larger areas of brush near deep water, a migration route, or some such feature, as discussed previously under "Stumps." When fishing this type of cover, it's best to get the lure into it; consequently, a keel fly or weedless bug usually will be in order, depending on how thick the cover is.

When fishing a shoreline, keep an eye peeled out in the lake for stickups, which often indicate slightly submerged cover. If you don't know whether a stickup indicates a single bush or a patch of brush, it will pay you to find out. Use a sinking weedless lure to feel out the area on all sides of the stickup. Many bass anglers are expert at using plastic worms to "read" cover and lake bottoms.

POCKETS AND DRAWS

Any pocket in the shoreline, or in such cover as grass beds, is worth casting into. How good a pocket is often depends on the depth of the water, and how many casts you make into a pocket depends largely on its size. Some draws will require a number of casts to fish them thoroughly.

In small pockets, say 1 foot wide and 3 feet deep, I usually make at least two casts—the first to the mouth, the second to the back of the pocket. Presenting the lure delicately and fishing it gently often is the key to catching bass in small pockets. A noisy approach may frighten the bass out of the pocket, especially if the water is shallow and clear. I might add that small pockets have been very productive for me, especially for largemouth.

COVES

In large impoundments and in some natural lakes, more fishing takes place in coves than in other places of comparable surface area. The reason isn't necessarily because more fish are in coves, but because the wind and water are normally calmer. This can be a big advantage to the fly caster, especially if he doesn't have a large, fully rigged bassboat; but calm water doesn't necessarily make for the best bass fishing.

It is, of course, usually advisable to pick coves carefully, looking for cover, structure, and substructure as discussed throughout this chapter and the next. I prefer coves with old creek channels running through them, or with vegetation or some such cover along the banks. Either new water from a creek or ample vegetation can raise the oxygen content of cove water to a level higher than that out in the main body of the lake or impoundment. Also, the temperature in a cove can vary considerably from that in the main lake; generally, a cove tends to warm up faster in spring and cool off faster in fall, which can mean that cove fishing is better during spring and fall, at least in some areas. But don't overlook the back end of coves on warm, sunny days during the dead of winter.

RUN-INS

Never neglect to cast to the mouth of a branch or drainage ditch. Bass often lie around such spots, especially after or during a rain, watching for food washing down. Often a change in water clarity, temperature, or oxygen content will attract and hold bass around a run-in. In brackish water, a change in salinity can attract bass. One of the hottest run-ins I ever saw was some sort of drainage, through a little ditch, on the Arkansas River in the city limits of Little Rock.

The mouths of canals and overflow ditches should also be fished, although they may be "run-outs." Causeway bridges or culverts in lakes and impoundments often have water flowing one way or the other, depending on wind and wave action. Fishing them accordingly will sometimes pay off.

BLUFFS AND LEDGES

Any bluff or ledge is likely to hold bass—especially spots. But bluffs and ledges are difficult to fish with a fly rod. If the bass are near the surface, the area can be fished normally. But remember that the water is likely to be quite deep, and that the bass may be in underlying pockets, so that surface lures may not do the trick.

If surface lures fail to produce, the best bet (with a fly rod) is to hold the boat close to the bluff and fish parallel to it. Try a weighted streamer or some such sinking lure; cast ahead of the boat and tight-line the lure down instead of retrieving it quickly. (Remember to watch your line carefully when fishing a sinking lure; a bass can engulf and blow out a lure without the angler ever knowing it. If your line twitches, set the hook.) On the next cast, place your lure 5 feet or so ahead of the first cast, and again tight-line the lure down. And so on from one end of the bluff to the other.

ROCKS

Any sort of rocky structure or bottom may attract bass, especially in lakes and impoundments where soft mud bottoms predominate. Always fish large single boulders and rock piles along the shore or in shallow water. (During a cold snap, partly submerged boulders can hold enough heat to warm the water around them.) Lake bottoms composed of gravel or cert may hold bass, especially if most of the lake bottom is mud; but it's better to have some sort of additional cover or structure.

See also the discussion of riprap under "Dams."

BOTTOM CHANGES

Be alert for any changes in the composition of a lake bottom, as, for example, where a mud bottom gives way to sand. It's best to have some sort of cover at the juncture, but this isn't absolutely necessary. I've caught bass in "clean" bare areas at lakeside homes. Often the composition and shape of the bank can provide tips on such bottom changes.

SUBMERGED MANMADE STRUCTURES

Usually, such structure as houses and barns that have been inundated are associated with deep, open water, but the bass angler should take advantage of any such structure along the shoreline. For example, old roadbeds entering the water might be good spots for bass, especially if old ditches are present on either side. Fencerows and old agricultural drainage ditches that slope into the water also can be very good spots to fish.

FISH ATTRACTORS

More and more state fish and game departments, as well as clubs and individuals, are sinking Christmas trees and other objects at strategic locations to attract bass and other fish. (One tackle company has even marketed an artificial tree with wide leaves.) The private attractors usually are hidden, but those paid for with government funds may be highly visible. Some of these will be in shallow water and should be fished, but, personally, I've never had much luck at these places, perhaps because they may attract more anglers than fish. The hidden structure will probably pay off better, if you can find it.

DOCKS, PIERS, BOATHOUSES, HOUSEBOATS, ETC.

Almost any sort of dock or other structure that extends out over the water provides good shade and cover for bass. Given a choice, I prefer to fish a dock at a vacation home rather than at a permanent residence. My thinking is that constant use tends to scare really big bass away. On the other hand, many people feed bread and table scraps to the fish. This draws bluegills, shiners, minnows, and such, which in turn draw bass.

Another reason for fishing around piers and docks is that people often sink down brush, old tires, and such stuff nearby. These "artificial reefs" are usually intended to draw crappie, but they're also excellent bass attractors. A fly rod isn't ideal for detecting this hidden structure, but it often can be located with deep diving plugs or with plastic worms fished on heavy sinkers. In fact, one of the main advantages of fishing plastic worms is that the expert can feel out the bottom. After locating the structure, the angler can remember its location for future trips with the fly rod.

Although I do fish piers and other such structures near a residence, I don't feel quite right about it. I've had too many people fishing in my backyard when I lived on a public lake, and more than once worm fishermen have banged heavy lead sinkers against my boat. I didn't really object to a bass angler fishing my backyard and moving on, but it rubbed me the wrong way for a guy to anchor 10 yards off my patio when I was out drinking my morning coffee. I didn't own the lake, though, and didn't have the gall of one of my neighbors, who came out the door in polka-dot pajamas saying, "Good morning, sports fans!" I have, however, run wire trotlines across my boat basin.

DAMS

Any dam, from farm ponds on up to huge impoundments, can provide excellent bass fishing. In the impoundments, pay particular attention to the spot where the dam joins the bank. If you're out in a boat and casting to a dam, try a soggy muddler minnow. Plop it a couple of times on the surface, then let it sink down while you make a slow retrieve so that the muddler bumps along the dam's surface.

Dams with riprap are especially good. The large rocks form pockets for crawfish, minnows, snakes, rats, and other bass food. Usually, the riprap slopes down at about 45 degrees. A slow-sinking eel or leech pattern (perhaps tied with a deer-hair head and a long supple tail) can work wonders. In addition to bass and other fish, I've also caught a 3-pound bullhead and a large snapping turtle while fishing riprap with slow-sinking lures.

In the fall of the year the bass may be quite shallow on the riprap, so that it can be fished successfully from the bank. A curve cast will sometimes help because it will permit you to retrieve the fly from shallow water to deeper water. (See chapter 15 for notes on the curve cast.)

POINTS

Some bass anglers more or less specialize in fishing points, and some of the tournament pros have made a career of it. The fly-rodder could do far worse, but fishing points thoroughly with a fly rod is more difficult than it is with spinning and baitcasting rigs, simply because the points that are visible from along the bank often extend far out into the lake or impoundment. Still, some very good surface and shallow fishing can be found along points. But one point may not be as good as another.

Consider the accompanying diagram. Point A might be good because, as shown by the contour lines, it extends out near the creek channel. Point B would likely be relatively unproductive. Point C could be a good spot for bass, but it would be easier to fish it properly with spinning or baitcasting gear by bumping a jig or other heavy lure down it—or up it.

Point D would likely hold bass because it's so close to the creek channel. Point E might be good because the lily pads and grass provide cover. The grass on the point extension should be fished thoroughly. Typically, I'll fish around the edge of grass points, then move in and fish the middle of it if I can get a keel streamer or weedless lure down in the water.

Point F is unlikely to be a good spot, but point G, also in shallow water, might be good because of the hard, rocky bottom.

In addition to land points, also keep an eye out for points in grass beds, weeds, stump fields, and so on.

Also, remember that bass tend to congregate at points, so that if you catch one there may be others. This is especially true of points near deep water, as at C and D. (If bass are at A or F, they'll likely be scattered and feeding instead of holding.) If

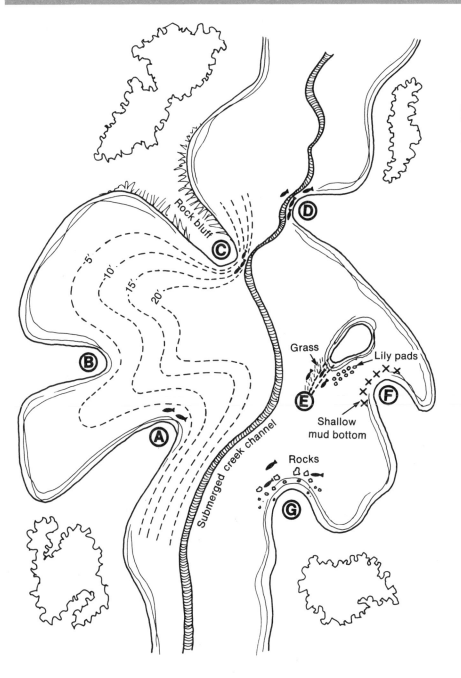

you do find a congregation of bass, don't spook them. Some bass experts have caught 70 or 80 pounds of lunker bass in short order from a single hot point!

CHAPTER 12

FISHING OPEN WATER

Anyone who takes a fly rod into midlake and starts casting randomly is pretty much wasting good fishing time. You might luck into a school of bass or some suspended bass, and you might even hit a veritable hot spot on the bottom. But it would be blind luck, and expert bass anglers proceed on more scientific footing.

Whichever way you choose to fish in open water—casting, trolling, or yo-yoing—locating structure and substructure is the key to success. A good depthfinder is almost indispensable, and a good topographic or contour map can save time, especially if you're fishing in a large man-made impoundment. Look especially for the following:

CREEK CHANNELS

Although creek channels submerged by impoundments are often difficult to fish thoroughly with a fly rod, they're one of the favorite types of structure among bass anglers. For one thing, they're relatively easy to find and follow because they're well marked on topographic maps.

There are several reasons why submerged creek channels are such good bass habitat:

- The creek, which ran through the area many years before it was impounded, probably has eroded the land or rock, making for drastic changes in depth.

- Creek channels usually provide both cover and shade.

- The channel is an excellent migration route from the main lake into the backside of associated coves.

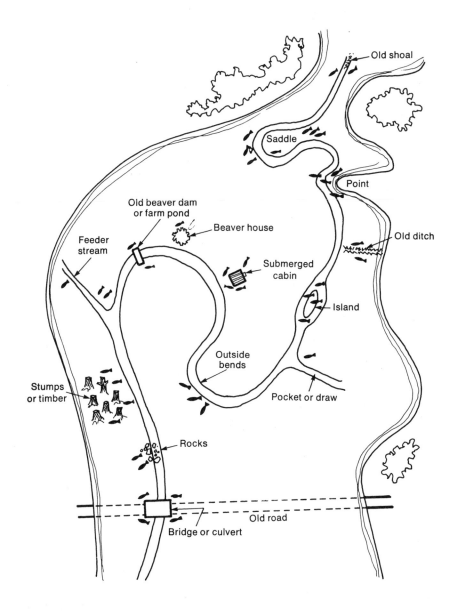

Submerged creek channel

- Because the creek channel existed before the impoundment was made, it is a natural spot for bass.

- The creek bed provides a break in the surrounding structure; if it ran through woods, for example, its sandbars, rock shoals, and so on contrast with the flooded timber or remaining stumps.

- The creek and river channels will be spots of maximum water flow in the impoundment.

If you want to fish a creek bed with your fly rod, remember that some parts of it may be better than others. It's best to concentrate on the outside bends and on the areas indicated on the accompanying diagram.

DEEP HOLES

Very often deep holes will attract bass, especially in natural lakes without much structure. Usually, a saucer-shaped hole without any substructure isn't ideal; a hole with a sharp drop on one or more sides is a better prospect. The area around the edge of the deep hole should be fished thoroughly; most of the large bass I've caught in natural lakes have been near, but not in, deep holes.

SUBMERGED ISLANDS

Any rise, knoll, or sunken island in a lake or impoundment may provide excellent bass fishing. In fact, I'd rather fish an island than a pothole. Knolls and islands are often especially productive if they occur in other structure, such as flooded timber or stump fields or creek channels. Sometimes you can find a knoll in a deep hole, and this can be a hot spot indeed.

Often an island will come to within a few feet of the surface, and such spots may prove to be prime bedding areas during spawning season. Some islands may have grass growing above the surface, and these are usually ideal for fly-rodding.

POINTS AND DRAWS

Any flooded point or draw can be a potential hot spot. Often, points that are visible on land will extend far out into a lake or impoundment.

SPRINGS

Underwater springs may be extremely good for bass, but they're difficult to locate. You may be able to find them indicated on some topographic maps.

ROCK BOTTOM

Rocky bottoms will hold bass, especially in a natural lake that is pretty much covered with mud and moss. In fact, any change in the bottom may attract bass, even far out in the lake.

LEDGES

Underwater ledges can sometimes be very good for bass, especially spots, but they're usually difficult to fish with a fly rod. Yo-yoing might work. Also, look for intense schooling activity when underwater ledges start near the surface.

TIMBER

Timber left standing in an impoundment often provides good bass fishing. If the bass are deep in heavy timber, about the only way to get a lure to them is by yo-yoing. Often, however, bass will be suspended in timber, so that even surface bugs and streamers may produce. Sputterbuzzing a spinner along the surface may be very effective at times for suspended bass. A good deal depends on how deep they are.

In large areas of timber, it's best to look for substructure or try to find a pattern. Such substructure might be a rise in the timber (caused by a knoll on the bottom), which can sometimes be detected without a depthfinder simply by looking at the height of the trees. A pattern might be established if, for example, you catch a bass from a certain kind of treetop or at a certain depth. Effective patterns may vary from day to day, or from one time of day to another.

MANMADE STRUCTURES

Submerged buildings, fencerows, roadbeds, bridges, culverts, dams from old farm ponds, etc., are excellent structure for bass. Bridges and culverts can be very good, but they're difficult to fish with a fly. Roadbeds are sometimes productive, and are easy to locate with the aid of depthfinders and topographic maps, or merely by noting where an old road enters or leaves an impoundment. When fishing roads, however, it's best to look for substructure or unusual features, such as sharp bends, S-curves, high road banks, hills, and so on.

DRAINAGE DITCHES

Many fields in river bottoms are flat and tended to be wet even before the impoundment was made, which means many of them have old drainage ditches running through them. These flooded ditches provide highways for bass to move into, out of, or across the fields when feeding or bedding. These old drainage ditches can provide some very good fishing. Often, topographic maps or aerial photos of the farm before impoundment will give you a clue.

STICKUPS

Any twig or limb sticking out of the water may indicate potentially good bass fishing. Stickups from submerged brush, willow trees, and so on should be of especial interest to fly-rodders because they indicate shallow water. Stickups in flats may be exceptionally good during the spawning season, and sometimes acre after acre of such flats are productive.

I'll usually start with poppers and other surface lures around stickups. If they don't produce, I'll tie on a keel fly and spinner, fishing 3 or 4 feet deep. If you want to go even deeper, try a weighted fly (or eel) and sinking line.

When you're fishing large areas of stickups in shallow water, it's best to move along pretty fast until you locate the bass.

FISH ATTRACTORS

As discussed in the previous chapter, fish attractors are becoming more and more common in our lakes and impoundments. These are often maintained by the fish and game departments of the various states, in which case they will usually be well marked so that the angler can spot them easily. Others are put out by individuals or by fishing clubs, and these are hard to find. The best bet is to spy on local anglers during bass tournaments, then mark the spot carefully by triangulation or some other means.

There is one type of openwater fishing that doesn't require a depthfinder, topographic maps, or other such aids, although you will need a fast boat: jump fishing for schooling bass. The idea is to ride around on the boat until you spot schooling activity, then run in close enough to cast, cut the motor, and start fishing as quickly as possible—before the school sounds.

Actually, the bass aren't really schooling; they're feeding on baitfish, usually shad. Consequently, jump fishing is usually better on lakes or impoundments with large shad populations. Schooling can also occur in rivers, although the action isn't usually good enough to justify jump fishing. Moreover, really good jump fishing is pretty much a southern sport, although bass do school to some extent in large lakes and impoundments north of the Mason–Dixon line.

Jump fishing can be good in spring, summer, and fall, depending on the particular impoundment or lake, and it is often better during the middle of the day. Consequently, if you plan to be on a lake all day and have a fast bassboat, you might bug the shoreline during early morning, chase the schools during the middle of the day, and return to the shoreline in late afternoon.

As I pointed out in chapter 6, it's often important to match whatever the schooling bass are feeding on, not only in profile but also in length. Streamers, bucktails, and ultralight spoons are in my opinion better than plugs, and this makes the fly rod a good choice for jump fishing. It's a different sort of casting, however, from working a shoreline or casting to cover. In jump fishing, distance is more important than accuracy. You should be able to shoot line out quickly, with a minimum of false casts, before the school sounds. It's best to keep the fly line neatly coiled on the boat deck, so that you'll be ready when the action starts. If you're serious about jump fishing, consider investing in a shooting head and a rod fitted with light, single-footed aluminum oxide rings. You might also consider a bassboat with a removable seat on the fishing deck. And then you might take a tip from Charles Waterman and put a plastic garbage can up there to hold your shooting line, if nobody is looking.

Polarized sunglasses will help you spot schooling activity, and binoculars will greatly extend your range. Also, be on the lookout for swooping gulls and other birds that feed on baitfish.

See chapter 6 for a discussion of lures, retrieves, and other matters that will help you catch schooling bass. I might add here that schooling bass will sometimes hit any reasonable offering, but if they don't hit whatever you're throwing them within three or four casts, try something else. I've seen guys, even fly-rodders, cast for an hour into a school of bass without a strike. It can be frustrating, to say the least.

W hen I first started outlining this book, I planned to put some simple beginner's casting instructions in an appendix and let it go at that. My thinking was that people who already know how to cast would be spared the details in the main body of the book. After watching dozens of bass anglers at work, however, I decided that casting instructions definitely should be a real part of the text itself and not stuck back in an appendix.

In addition to instructing rank beginners, I hope that the following chapters will

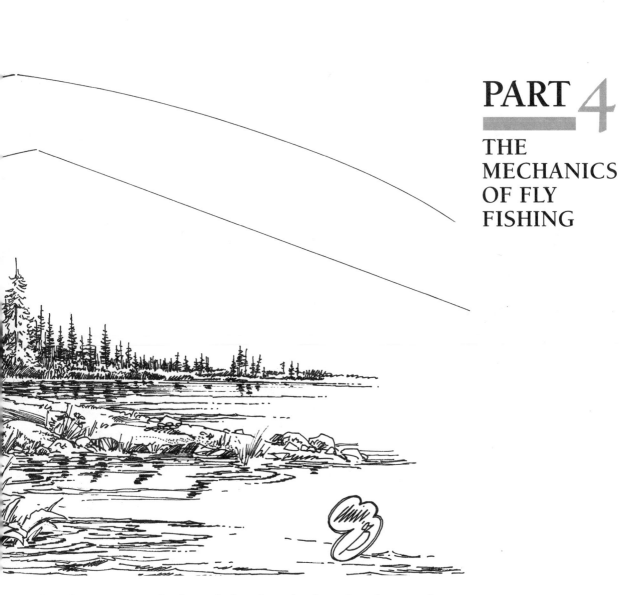

PART 4

THE MECHANICS OF FLY FISHING

help make casting easier for those who have been thrashing about for years. Casting a fly for normal fishing distances should be an almost effortless process. If you find that fly casting tires you quickly, either you don't have balanced tackle or you need to work on your style. Also, some trout anglers and bluegill buggers may have trouble switching to large flies and bugs. Sometimes this is merely a matter of equipment (usually the leader) or a matter of habit and timing. A large, wind-resistant bug is hard to turn over and slows down the cast.

CHAPTER 13

CASTING A LINE

Perhaps the best way to learn to cast is to attend a good school or to get some personal guidance from an expert. But this isn't necessary. In fact, I learned to cast a fly rod by simply buying an outfit, carefully reading the manufacturer's booklets, and starting to cast. I might add that I was catching fish (bluegill, mostly) on my rig within two hours after I put a line on the reel. To be sure, I wasn't getting distance or shooting line, and my style left a lot to be desired, but the fact remains that I was casting a bug and catching fish. Fortunately, I did receive some good advice shortly thereafter from a competent fly caster who watched me in action.

I think I picked up elementary fly casting easily because:

1. I had formed reasonably good habits with spinning and baitcasting rigs.
2. I believed the fly-casting instructions.
3. I tried to analyze what went wrong on an unsuccessful cast so that I could do better next time.

If my experience at teaching others to cast is any indication, some anglers have trouble with a fly rod because:

1. They acquired bad habits from baitcasting and spinning.
2. They don't understand the principles of fly casting and therefore don't fully believe the instructions.
3. After an unsuccessful cast they merely try harder to force the bug out instead of stopping to think about what they're doing, or not doing.
4. They have inadequate equipment, especially the leader.

Once I tried to teach a stubborn fellow (my older brother) how to cast a bug. After he had watched me make a couple of casts from the front seat of the boat, he said it didn't look like there were much to it. (There isn't.) He took the rod, snatched the bug out of the water, slung the rod behind him, and swished it forward. Line, leader, and bug collapsed in a heap onto the water short of the mark. I told him that he hadn't stopped the rod overhead and hadn't waited for the line to straighten out on the backcast. He stood up, snatched the line out of the water, slung the rod over his shoulder, and put all the muscle he had into the forward cast, determined to sling that damned bug out. Since he got the backcast off to a bad start, this cast was even more disastrous. Line and leader and bug fell all over the boat. I repeated my instructions, but he didn't pay any attention and kept flogging away. I said no more until he convinced himself that he couldn't get the bug out. Once he accepted the fact that he needed help, we started over and he was casting fairly well within a few minutes.

Most of the casting instructions I've seen advise the beginner to practice on a smooth, freshly cut lawn or some such surface with 80 feet or so of clearance. This is probably sound advice, but I learned on the water simply because I lived beside a lake and had trees all over my yard. I consider water to be the ideal place to learn casting. Why? The water's surface tensions the line during the pickup, thereby helping to load the rod for the backcast. I didn't realize this at first and I was once somewhat embarrassed when a manufacturer asked me to try out his new rod. We were standing in a slick asphalt parking lot that was covered lightly with sand. In short, I couldn't cast the rod very well. On the water, it would probably have worked nicely. I advise beginners to start on the water or wet grass. I also advise beginners to start with a small fly instead of a large bug—and snip off the business end of the hook.

Although the motion involved in fly casting should be fluid rather than jerky, for the sake of discussion it can be broken down into steps and phases. I'll discuss these in detail later, but first I'd like to run through a simple cast with the aid of a clock-face diagram. (A guy who teaches fly casting reports that he had some young students recently who didn't have a clue what clock positions were. It seems they've grown up with digital watches!)

Work out about 30 feet of fly line straight in front of you (for a first practice cast, simply strip the line off the reel and walk it out if on land or wading, or move away from it if you're on a boat). With the rod at 9 o'clock and pointed pretty much

The Backcast

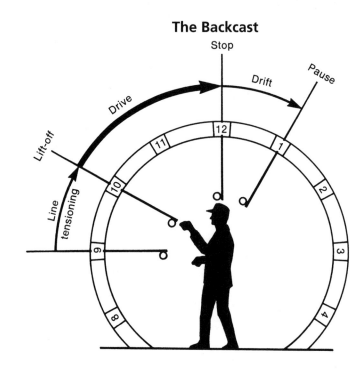

The Forward Cast

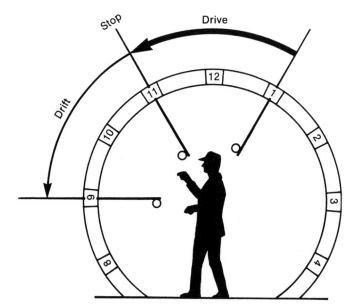

toward the fly, start the pickup by raising the rod tip progressively. When the tip is at about 10 o'clock, *accelerate* the rod, picking up the line and casting it overhead. Continue this power stroke to the 12 o'clock position, then *stop* the rod. Stop it dead, directly over your head. *Pause* until the line straightens out behind you, allowing the rod to drift back to about 1 o'clock. (Expert distance casters may drift back as far as 3 o'clock, but beginners should stop at 1 o'clock.) When you feel the line load the rod, *drive* the rod forward to 11 o'clock. The fly line shoots forward, carrying the leader and lure with it. The line turns over on the forward cast and on the backcast, forming a loop that unrolls the length of the line.

The backcast is the key to casting with a fly rod, and a good backcast almost assures a passable forward cast. But remember that the backcast isn't complete unless the line straightens out behind you. If you pause too long, however, the line and leader will touch down. Although a number of fish and possibly a water skier or two have been caught by default on the backcast, you'll do well to keep the line above the water and out of the bushes.

Anyhow, the simple instructions given above are all you'll need to start casting a fly or bug, provided your gear is matched pretty well. If you stick with just such simple instructions, however, you might form a few bad habits that you'll later regret. Here are the various phases and steps of the cast, together with some related topics, in detail.

THE GRIP

Hold the rod firmly, but not tensely, in the right hand (left if you are left-handed). Most fly-rodders place the thumb on top of the handle, but a few anglers prefer to have the thumb at the side, and some who use short rods and light lines find that they can present a tiny dry fly more delicately with the index finger on top of the handle. Any grip that is comfortable throughout the cast is all right, but I do recommend that the thumb be on top of the handle.

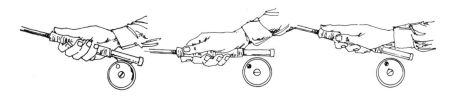

Three possible finger positions on the rod handle

THE PIVOT POINTS

Using the wrist as a pivot point is extremely tiring if you make repeated casts with gear heavy enough to handle large bass bugs. Although some trout anglers who work small streams may cast with the wrist, most modern casters keep the wrist stiff (except when the rod is drifting). Thus, the rod becomes an extension of the forearm and the elbow becomes the pivot point; the cast is made with the arm muscles, which are both long and strong compared with the short muscles brought into play by a flick of the wrist.

I recommend that beginners keep their elbow at their side during the cast, but this isn't a hard and fast rule. Many experts raise the elbow during the cast, especially if they're going for distance. I feel, however, that the angler who gets his regular casting down pat will unconsciously modify or adjust the elbow movement as required. Note that even if the expert caster raises the elbow, it's still the pivot point for the forearm and rod, even though its position has changed. Anyhow, until you get your timing down pat, it's best to practice with your elbow at your side.

MAKING THE BACKCAST

Too many bass anglers snatch their bugs off the water instead of picking them up smoothly. The trick is to start the lure moving until the rod is at about 10 o'clock, then lift it off with a smooth, accelerating power stroke. Continue this movement—an upward lift, forceful, with a stiff wrist—until the rod is directly overhead. Then stop the rod. Some anglers, probably the majority, actually stop the rod at the 1 o'clock position or even later, but the beginner will do well to concentrate on 12 o'clock, sharp. (You're likely to wind up at 1 or 2 o'clock anyway.) In time this stop will come naturally, and I suspect that the ideal stopping point will vary slightly not only from angler to angler but also with various rods and lines. When I'm casting with my 1¾-ounce graphite rod, I actually stop at a few minutes before 12; with my 6¼-ounce fiberglass rod, I normally stop at a little after 12.

Most accomplished anglers let the rod drift back to 1 o'clock, or even 2, 3, or 4 o'clock, but this movement is only a drift, doesn't exert any force on the line, and occurs only after a definite stop, although it may appear to be a continuous power stroke to an untrained eye.

Note: All the motions and the application of power from the pickup until the stop are not directed toward casting the line behind you, but instead are focused on casting the line high into the air. This helps with making the stop, and will keep the backcast up where it ought to be.

THE PAUSE AND DRIFT

After stopping the rod directly overhead, you must pause while the line straightens out behind you. If you begin the forward cast too early, your backcast will be aborted and your rod won't load properly. In effect, this is similar to putting a spinning or baitcasting plug on the ground with several feet of slack line, and then trying to cast it out. If the plug doesn't load the rod, you can't cast it effectively; if the fly line doesn't load the rod, you can't cast it effectively either, no matter how hard you try.

The length of the pause will vary with the amount of line out, the weight and wind resistance of the lure, and other factors. This is not a stopwatch matter. When the line straightens out, it exerts a discernible tug on the rod. The experienced angler senses this and then automatically begins the forward stroke. Beginners often have difficulty here; they don't quite get the message and pause too long or, as more often happens, they don't wait long enough. The best bet is to look over your shoulder and watch the line straighten out. Soon you'll gain confidence and will believe the slight tug when you feel it. (Also remember that timing can be different from one bug to another, depending on wind resistance.)

After you get the stop and the pause down pat, you'll probably start opening your wrist slightly to permit the rod to drift back. You might also raise your elbow, in a sort of arm-cocking motion in anticipation of the forward cast, especially if you have to make a long or difficult cast into the wind. I think that both of these motions are natural and shouldn't be of too much concern to the beginner. At first, concentrate on the 12 o'clock stop and the pause.

THE FORWARD CAST

It has been said that if you make a good backcast, a decent forward cast will be almost automatic. There's a lot of truth in the statement, but the forward cast shouldn't be taken for granted.

A common mistake is to bring the rod down instead of forward. A downward stroke applies the power while the rod is going through a wide arc, which results in the line forming a wide loop. A wide loop is indicative of a slow, inaccurate cast that isn't good for getting distance or going into the wind.

Anyhow, the better way is to drive the rod forward and keep the arc narrow. Stop the rod at about 11 o'clock, then open the wrist and let the rod drift down to about 9:30 while the line is straightening out.

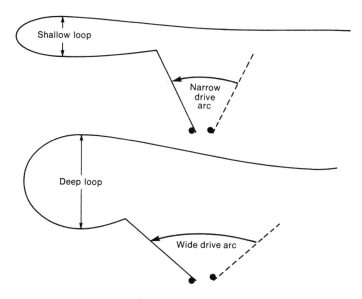

The hammer analogy is often used to illustrate the forward power stroke, and I would like to repeat it here, briefly. Stand a foot and a half back from a wall, and start driving in a nail at eye level. From this position, you'd first draw the hammer back over your shoulder to about 1 o'clock and then drive it forward until it hit the nail and stopped at about 11 o'clock. Try it, and remember the analogy when you practice your forward stroke. (Actually, the hammer analogy also applies to the backcast, except that you would be hitting a nail slightly behind your head.)

The forward stop is important for casting a fast line, although the principle is a little difficult to understand fully. For one thing, stopping the rod at 11 o'clock keeps the arc narrow and the loop tight—but there's more to it than that. I think it's safe to say that the stop forces the rod to "unload," which in turn accelerates the fly line.

RELEASING LINE

Throughout the cast, the left hand should keep the line under tension and should pretty much follow the movements of the rod hand. If you want to shoot line for a longer cast, the time to do so is at the completion of the forward power stroke. The line to be released, of course, must be stripped off the reel and should be loose at your feet, held loosely in your line hand, or coiled in a stripping basket. Most bass anglers keep a goodly length of working line off their reel, and they adjust the length of their casts by stripping in line before the backcast or by shooting line out with the forward cast.

If you want to release more line than you can shoot out on the cast, you can do so by false-casting. To make a false cast, proceed with the backcast and forward cast as normal, but pick the line up for another cast before the lure or line touches down. The idea, of course, is to release line on each false cast until you can get the bug out as far as you want it. False casts can also be used to dry out flies and deer-hair bugs, if you want them dry.

PRESENTING THE LURE

After getting the basics of casting down pat, you'll slowly discover that the fly rod is more accurate than a spinning rig. You might also discover that you can present the lure more gently than you can with either baitcasting or spinning gear, and the comparatively light weight of the bass bug or fly isn't the only reason.

I feel that accuracy will come in time, but gentle presentation may not. The trick is to aim the bug a foot or so above the target. If you aim right at the target, say a small pocket in lily pads, the bug will shoot in and splat down. If you aim high and the cast goes well, your line will go out with the leader and bug following. Toward the end of the cast, the fly line will straighten out, transmitting the energy to the leader. The leader and bug will turn over and all the energy will be expended in midair, just over the pocket. The bug will simply alight on the water. It's beautiful. Pure poetry, and all that. More important, such a presentation is likely to attract a bass instead of spooking it, especially in shallow water. But remember that in deeper water it might sometimes be best to splash the bug down to attract attention.

FANCY PICKUPS

I'm fond of fishing my bug or lure on the pickup, and therefore I usually avoid anything fancy. At times, however, a normal pickup will get you in trouble or just won't do the job. If, for example, you cast over a partly submerged log, a normal pickup may well hang up your bug. The same problem may occur if your fly line gets under a lily pad, or if you cast into rather thick grass. Here are a few tricks to try when the need arises.

The snake pickup. Start this move by holding the rod out in front of you and parallel to the water. Wave the tip from side to side just before and during the pickup. This sends S-curves down the line, and these curves will lift leader and lure out of the water on the pickup.

The half-roll pickup. Start a roll cast as described in chapter 15. While the lure and leader are in the air toward the end of the roll, make a regular pickup for the backcast. (When making the roll, don't let the rod drift down past 10:30 after applying the power stroke.) The half-roll pickup is excellent for getting a sinking line out of the water in preparation for a regular pickup.

The snap pickup. Hold the rod at 10 o'clock and raise it to 11. Then snap it back to 10. This movement will send a hump down the line, which in turn will lift the lure off the water. At that point, you pick up as usual for the backcast. The snap pickup is very good for getting flies and bugs over obstructions.

I would like to suggest that some bass anglers make too many casts that are too short. Casts of, say, only 20 feet will tire you more quickly than normal casts of 40 feet, simply because you don't have enough fly line out to load the rod properly. Fly rods are designed to carry the first 30 or 35 feet of a fly line; with less line out the rod is simply underloaded—like trying to cast a ¼-ounce lure with a baitcasting rod designed for ½-ounce lures.

Short casts are sometimes necessary, of course, as when fishing some small streams. But many bass anglers, when they begin to tire from repeated casts, tend to inch their boats in closer to the bank or cover when they might actually cast with less effort if they got farther out. They'll catch more bass, too, by making casts of normal length—especially if they're standing or fishing from a bassboat with high, deck-mounted pedestal seats.

CHAPTER 14

GETTING DISTANCE AND BEATING THE WIND

The most enjoyable way to fish a bug with a fly rod is to make casts of about 40 feet, and normally this is all the distance you'll need. It isn't too difficult to cast even a large bug farther than 40 feet, but it becomes tiring to pick up and cast a lot of fly line for fast, repeated cycles, especially since floating bass bugs are rarely fished more than a few feet before the pickup, which means that you'll make lots of casts per hour. Subsurface lures, of course, can be fished on in, but retrieving a surface bug more than 3 or 4 feet is pretty much a waste of time. Even if you do retrieve a bass bug in close, you'll have to false-cast to get it out again. So, working the boat along about 40 feet out from the shoreline or cover saves you a lot of time and effort.

But it's good to know how to make longer casts should the need arise. Casting

70, 80, or even 100 feet isn't unreasonable if you have adequate, balanced gear and aren't trying to throw the largest bug in your tackle box. The secret is in increasing line speed, keeping a tight loop, and learning to handle shooting line smoothly.

Experienced casters use several tricks to increase line speed without overly exerting themselves, but I'd like to emphasize at this point that the quickest road to distance casting is learning to cast 40 feet of line effortlessly. Once you get things down pat, you can start working on your distance. It is definitely a mistake to get too fancy too soon.

INCREASING LINE SPEED

As I said in the last chapter, I think the best way to learn to cast is to keep your elbow pretty much at your side unless you have good reason for bringing it up. Learning in this manner helps to stop the rod overhead; if you hold the elbow down and keep the wrist stiff, you *have* to stop the rod correctly. But for distance casting you may want to get a longer drive stroke, and there are other occasions when you need to raise the elbow considerably.

One way to increase the total rod-forward movement without increasing the arc is to raise your elbow up and out, then drive the whole rod straight ahead. One of the best illustrations I've seen of this principle appeared in a booklet by Scientific Anglers years ago, and they gave their permission to reprint it (I have modified the drawing a little). Note that the hand and the entire rod move forward, and the direction of applied force is almost in a straight line. You simply raise your elbow on the backcast, pause for the line tug, and drive the rod forward and straight ahead; then you tip the

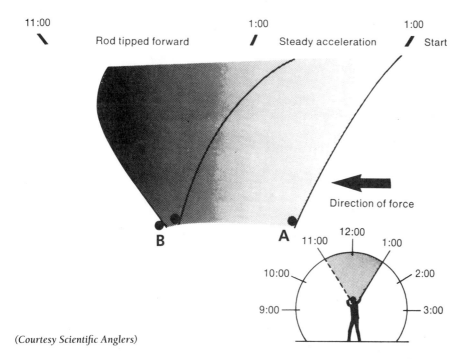

(Courtesy Scientific Anglers)

rod forward sharply with wrist movement and thumb pressure. Note carefully that the arc described by the rod is still from 1 o'clock to 11—although the "clock dial" itself moves forward. During the movement from A to B, the rod remains cocked in the 1 o'clock position. What this movement does is increase the length of the power stroke while keeping the arc narrow and the loop tight.

I might add that Scientific Anglers recommended this cast as standard, whether you want to cast 30 feet or 100. Further, they recommended that you start casting using this basic procedure. A good argument might be made for this, and you could do a good deal worse. But personally, I find this cast more tiring for normal distances than the old "elbow at the side" cast. I also have trouble holding the rod vertical and then tipping it with wrist movement. So when I use this method, I usually start the arc and continue it during the entire stroke. But this is the sort of thing you'll need to work out for yourself as you gain experience.

No matter whether you move the elbow or keep it put, you can definitely increase line speed by stopping sharply at the end of the power stroke, both on the backcast and on the forward cast. Emphatically stopping the rod causes the tip to spring forward (or back on the backcast), thereby unloading the rod. If you don't take advantage of the energy stored in the rod, then you are, at least in part, slinging the line instead of casting it. The same thing is true of casting with spinning or baitcasting rods, and, I might add, most anglers do tend to sling either a lure or a fly line. Although they can surely catch bass by so doing, they're just making it harder on themselves.

In addition to making full use of the stop, some experts go a step further with a wrist flick and thumb pressure at the end of the forward power stroke. This is difficult to describe, but I would call it a sort of double-clutching movement. What they do is stop the rod arm, then emphasize the tip movement with the wrist and thumb. Still other anglers tip the rod back a bit after making the stop and before releasing the shooting line; this backward tip apparently accelerates the forming of the loop and keeps it tighter.

LINE HAULS

Although good casting form and habits together with a few tricks will enable you to cast long distances, the best way to increase line speed is to use line hauls. Normally, the line hand more or less follows the rod hand, maintaining tension on the line. When making a haul, the line hand not only maintains the necessary tension but also pulls the line. Although most fly-rodders with any experience use a line haul of sorts on the pickup and backcast, the principle is fully realized only in the double haul. It isn't easy. It requires study, concentration, good timing, and practice.

The double haul is primarily an aid to distance casting, and it really isn't required unless you want to make long casts. The bass angler, however, can use hauls to advantage when casting heavy bugs for shorter distances, and I find a double haul especially useful for casting bugs into a strong head wind. Also, hauls made with the left hand can, if the rhythm is right, take some of the load off the casting arm, which can be important during a hard day's bass fishing. If you're interested in becoming adept at taking bass on the fly, I recommend that you learn how to make hauls, and that you practice them during your routine fishing, just to get the timing down pat.

1. Start the double haul by grasping the line out in front of you.
2. Bring the rod up for the power stroke and haul the line down with the line hand.
3. When the rod is stopped, the line hand has hauled down quite a length of line.
In an actual cast, the line hand would be behind your hip pocket.

4. While the rod is drifting back during the pause, the line hand feeds the line through the rod guides.
5. After the backcast has straightened out and you have fed out the line, start a forceful forward cast and haul the line down sharply.
6. After completing the power stroke for the forward cast, release line for shooting.

Personally, I almost always make a single haul of sorts when casting with a fly rod. On the pickup, the line hand grasps the line near the stripping guide. As the rod hand is raised, the line hand hauls down. This aids in the pickup simply because it helps get the line moving; and it speeds up the line during the power stroke of the backcast. So far this is pretty simple, and most anglers who do a lot of fly casting make some sort of single haul on the pickup, whether or not they realize it. This is especially true of anglers who work a shoreline or otherwise make repeated casts.

Anyhow, the double haul starts with a relatively simple single haul on the pickup. Assume that you've pulled in a yard of line with the single haul. As soon as you complete the power stroke of the backcast, and while drifting the rod back, feed this yard of line, while maintaining a slight tension on it, back through the rod guides. Your line hand sort of follows the rod and may extend almost to the stripping guide. The fly line, of course, is straightening out behind you, so that feeding the line isn't difficult once you've mastered the timing. If you watch your backcast over your shoulder, you'll get a better feeling for what's going on. A high, fast backcast will help things go smoothly.

After you've fed the line through the rod guides, bring the rod forward and haul the line back down. The rod hand stops the forward stroke and the line hand drops the line. The rod drifts down and the running line shoots through the guides. (Some anglers try not to release the shooting line until they feel a slight forward tug; others drop the line immediately upon completing the forward power stroke.)

It might seem ridiculous to haul in line with your line hand when you're trying to cast it out with your rod hand, but the purpose of the haul is to increase line speed. If things work right, you can shoot out much more line than you hauled in. The greater the line speed, the more distance you can get when shooting.

There is a good bit of leeway on the distance and the intensity of the haul. It might be merely a tug on the line, or, if you're shooting for distance, you might haul the line forcefully for almost 6 feet, ending up with your line hand back beyond your hip pocket! If photographed at the right time, some distance experts would look more like discus throwers than fly casters!

I almost have to add that many distance casters disregard the classic clock-dial casting directions, and certainly don't hold the 12 and 1 o'clock positions as sacred. Some of them let the rod drift back almost horizontally. For other points of view, see *Longer Fly Casting*, by Lefty Kreh; and *Joan Wulff's Fly Casting Techniques*, by Joan Salvato Wulff.

A specialist at distance shooting can work out 30 feet of shooting taper and then get out 100 feet in short order. The problem is what to do with the 70 feet of running line—how to keep it from tangling, how to get it through the guides properly, and how to keep it ready to shoot at all times. If you're on a boat with a casting deck, you can carefully coil the line before you make the cast, or, if you're wading, you can carefully put it into a stripping basket. Some anglers even loop it over some sort of clip on their waders or hold coils in their mouth. All this is fine if you don't make fast, repeated casts; you can coil your line ahead of time and be ready. But the bass angler needs to keep his bug in the water, and all that line just gets in the way—especially if you have a foot pedal on the deck that controls the bow-mounted fishing motor.

In short, I don't think that shooting heads and long running lines are practical for bass fishing. The exceptions might include jump fishing and the use of lead-core shooting heads for fishing structure in deep water.

Anyhow, if you plan to do a lot of distance shooting, you'll need to work out some method of holding the line coiled properly.

WIND

Wind causes problems for fly casters, and a lot of anglers either quit fishing or look for secluded spots when the going gets rough. No one can fish in a hurricane, but normal wind speeds up to 20 miles an hour can be overcome; in fact, bass fishing is often better with some chop on the water. My personal policy is to fish where I think the bass are if my electric fishing motor will handle the boat. In other words, it's boathandling problems, not wind-related casting problems, that cause me to quit a hot spot. I do, however, usually make shorter casts in a stiff breeze. For one thing, the bass can't see the angler or boat as readily through chop.

One way to beat the wind is to keep your cast low. Wind speeds often will be greater a few feet above your head, especially if you're fishing along a wooded shoreline. Regular overhead casts can be made in wind, but in most cases it's best to keep your line low and your loop tight. A side cast (discussed in the next chapter) will help, and it's often possible to make a horizontal side cast, in which rod and line get only a few feet off the water. Side casts are rather limited on distance, however, and it's difficult for two anglers to make side casts off the same boat.

Another way to beat the wind is to increase the line speed by any of the methods discussed earlier in this chapter. Note also that the weight and wind resistance of a bug or fly affects line speed, and often merely changing lures will solve some casting problems.

If I have a choice, I prefer to cast into head winds instead of casting with tail winds. A tail wind makes the backcast awkward and complicates your timing; the wind impedes the backcast so that the line doesn't load the rod properly, making it difficult to detect the little tug that signals you to proceed with the forward cast. A head wind, on the other hand, helps the backcast and emphasizes the line tug at the end of the pause. After you have a good backcast going for you, it's fairly easy to drive even a bass bug into a stiff head wind, provided that your gear is heavy enough and is reasonably matched. A line haul on the forward stroke helps a lot when you're driving a bug into a head wind. In any case, casting into a head wind causes no timing problems, and all you have to learn is how to drive the bug.

Generally, it's best to keep the backcast high and the forward cast low. Keeping the backcast up puts the wind to good use, and keeping the forward cast low will, at least at times, put the bug down under the stronger winds. Such a cast will tend to splat the bug down onto the water instead of presenting it gently, however; but a gentle presentation isn't too important when there's some chop on the water.

A strong head wind can cause some problems when you're trying to shoot for distance. The best bet is to increase line speed and keep the forward cast low with a very tight loop; don't release the shooting line until the rod has drifted down almost to the horizontal position.

When casting with a tail wind, remember that your backcast will have to be made into the wind; consequently, you'll need to keep the backcast low—and fast. A low backcast together with the tail wind, however, causes the line and fly to return too close to the angler on the forward cast, and more than one fly-rodder has wrapped the line around himself in a stiff tail wind. The best bet is to make the backcast with the rod at about a 45-degree angle from the vertical; in other words, make the backcast with a modified side cast. This keeps the line lower while at the same time permitting a shallow loop. After making such a backcast, bring the rod to vertical (during the pause) and make a high forward cast. The reason for making a high forward cast is to put the line up into the wind so that it will nudge along the cast. Such a "floating" cast isn't quite as accurate as a normal cast, but it's probably the best way to cope with a strong tail wind. Speeding up the backcast with a line haul and some muscle will help.

Finally, you might try facing the wind, making a false cast into it, and then fishing on your "backcast." This method will often work if accuracy isn't too important.

A crosswind that blows the line away from you doesn't cause too much of a problem. If you cast with your right hand, the wind would be blowing in from your left (or the reverse for southpaws). Distance and accuracy may be impaired, but a crosswind can usually be allowed for.

An adverse crosswind is another matter. I'm talking about a wind that tends to blow the line and lure back into you. If you're right-handed, a wind blowing in strong from your right will catch the line and cause the fly or bug to zip past dangerously close to your ear. It's very important to watch your business and somehow keep the line downwind. A backhand cast will work, or you might make an overhead cast by raising your casting arm high for the backcast, then letting your arm drift down a little to the left during the pause. When you make the power stroke, the line and lure come by on your left. In other words, the fly comes by on your right on the backcast, and returns on your left during the forward cast. Personally, I've never cared much for this cast, and I would just as soon have a bug in my right ear as in my left.

The best bet is to avoid steady casting in this type of crosswind. Most bass anglers fishing from boats with bow-mounted electric motors can merely change directions, putting the crosswind to the other side. Instead of fishing down a shoreline, fish up it, or vice versa. Why fight a crosswind for two or three hours? Anglers fishing on streams will have to live with crosswinds at times, but most bass streams bend around and offer good fishing on either side, so that the angler isn't continuously fighting an adverse crosswind. Besides, wind isn't usually as much of a problem on bass streams as it is on a large lake or impoundment.

I would like to emphasize that large, wind-resistant bass bugs are dangerous, with or without winds. I didn't realize just how dangerous until my daughter got a bug stuck in her eye. Fortunately, the hook merely buried up under the lid and didn't penetrate the eyeball—but we didn't know that during the long ride back to the boat landing and during the 22-mile drive to the nearest hospital emergency room. We were lucky.

CHAPTER 15

FISHING STREAMS AND TIGHT PLACES

Most of the information in Part Three on when and where to catch bass applies to fishing in large streams and small. Oxygen content, temperature, wind, and so on aren't quite as variable on streams as they are on large lakes and impoundments, and therefore aren't normally as much of a factor to be reckoned with. But bass in a stream prefer cover and shade just as surely as they do anywhere else. Stumps, logs, pockets, run-ins, and so on are just as important in streams as they are in natural lakes and impoundments. So is deep water, and the larger bass will often be in or near deep holes.

One difference with stream bass, however, is how the current affects their choice of feeding or holding areas. Bass in streams are fond of hanging out in eddies near swift water, perhaps behind a boulder at the end of a shoal run. In general, however, bass don't hang out in really swift water. But any change in flow, such as an eddy hole, may hold bass, and should be fished thoroughly, as should the interface between fast water and slow. Always remember that bass will usually be facing the current. Plan your approach and place your casts accordingly.

Apart from knowing where the fish are and which way they'll be pointing, the big difference in fly-rodding for bass on a stream is primarily a matter of mechanics. Casting is more difficult on some streams because of trees along the bank, and the current working against the large fly line causes problems in fishing a bug, streamer, or other lure properly. Here are some tricks that will help.

ROLL CAST

Often on streams, and sometimes on lakes, you won't have enough room behind you to make a backcast. The roll cast usually will work in this situation, since it requires no backcast at all. Although it isn't great for distance or accuracy, you can, after a few practice casts, get a bug out 40 feet or so, and practice will improve your accuracy. I recommend that you make a roll cast from time to time even when you don't need it.

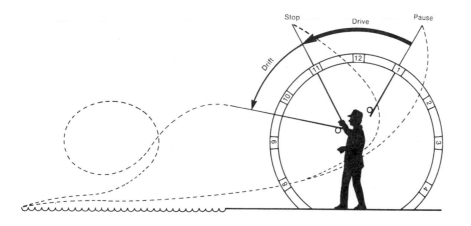

Proceed by raising the rod slowly to the 1:00 position. Pause briefly, until the line comes to a full stop on the water, then drive the rod with an accelerating motion to 11:00. Stop. Emphasize the stop. Then let the rod drift down nearly to vertical.

If you want a little more distance on a roll cast, you can shoot some line immediately after the stop. Or you can work out a little line when you're raising the rod tip to 1:00, but remember that the line must not be allowed to go slack.

You can make roll casts with sinking line and light streamers or bucktails as well as with floating lines and bugs. The procedure is pretty much the same, except maybe for raising the rod tip a little faster when you're getting ready to cast a sinking line.

A roll can also be used at times to unsnag a bug or fly, and a roll pickup often can help get a lure out of grass and thick cover. Some anglers also use a roll to get a sinking line or sinking tip up near the surface before proceeding with a regular pickup.

STEEPLE CAST

Often there'll be too many obstructions behind you for a normal cast, but not enough to require a roll cast. If you use your full arm and make a quick pickup, emphasizing an upward thrust, you can throw the fly line almost straight up. Then you can start the forward cast without much of a pause. Actually, the forward cast requires very little power; instead, the rod is used to sort of direct the downward fall of the line. If you do make a powerful forward stroke, your line and bug will splat down heavily into the water. Instead of a power stroke, try dropping the arm down and drifting the rod forward.

POCKET CAST

It's always a good idea to know what's behind you when you're fishing a stream or other tight spots. One trick that often works is to find an opening in the trees behind you and cast to it. This can be done by looking over your shoulder on the backcast, or even by facing the pocket, casting to it, and presenting the lure on the "backcast."

FLOP CAST

When drifting down a small stream on a boat, or proceeding upstream with the aid of an electric motor, I'll often merely flop the lure from one bank to the other. Typically, I'll fish the lure for only 2 or 3 feet before flopping it over to the other side. I've gone a mile or more up or down a bushy stream without making a single backcast! The flop cast can be made from overhead or from the side. I usually hold my rod forward off the bow of the boat and flick the lure from one bank to the other. This technique works best in rather sluggish streams averaging 50 to 60 feet across. The boat, of course, should be kept in midstream.

SIDE CAST

Here's a cast you can use when there's no space for an overhead cast; for example, when you're standing under a tree. Use the regular casting cycle, but simply hold the rod at an angle instead of vertical. I often use a horizontal side cast to get bugs and flies under overhanging brush. It's also a useful cast to make in high wind, but it's rather limited in distance.

BACKHAND CAST

This cast can be made by holding the rod at some angle across your body. The angle can vary from almost vertical to almost horizontal. The backhand cast can be used in wind, or when obstructions make an overhead cast impossible.

CURVE CAST

A curve cast can be helpful in current to hold line mending to a minimum. The object of the curve cast is to curve the line upstream of the lure so that the current won't quickly pull your bug or fly out of position.

Of more interest to the average bass angler, the curve cast also helps get a bug back behind stumps and other cover, or into pockets that would be inaccessible by a regular overhead forward cast. I like the curve cast for getting under boat docks and for fishing riprap from the bank. (The curve cast leaves the fly line out in the water with the leader and lure curving in toward the bank. With a slow retrieve, the lure works out from the bank toward the lake.) I almost always use what is sometimes called a *positive curve,* in which the line ends up being pretty much straight out in front of you, and the bug overshoots the mark. The trick is to make a side-armed cast, aiming to the left of the target, and then stopping the cast and pulling back toward the end. This straightens the line, but causes the bug and leader to flop around toward the target.

LINE MENDING

A stream's current can cause some pretty severe problems at times. Assume, for example, that you cast across the stream to a likely looking eddy hole. Your bug turns over just right and you want to fish the hole with a very slow twitch-and-rest motion. Unfortunately, the faster current midstream will likely catch your fly line, quickly forming a belly and dragging your bug away from the hole you want to fish. Line mending will help keep the bug in position a little longer.

The trick is simply to hold the rod out in front of you and roll it and the line upstream, using your forearm, with the wrist held stiff. The difficult thing is controlling the roll so that you don't pull the bug out of position, and I personally find this hard to do. In general, however, the tricks of line mending are not as important in bass angling as in trout fishing.

Most anglers who fish streams with a boat or tube merely drift with the current, simply because drifting or floating is the easiest way to go. Floating from one bridge or access point to another is by far the most popular way to fish some streams. If you want to slow the drift, get about 5 feet of heavy chain and tie it to a line, then drag it like an anchor—letting out line to slow the boat, taking in line to speed up. The chain will occasionally hang up on bottom, but it will usually snake over or through surprisingly thick log jams, rocks, and other debris. I do have reservations about dragging a chain over a hard bottom, however, because it may make undesirable sounds, which carry for long distances downstream.

Anglers with electric motors on their boats have a choice of fishing upstream or down if the motor is powerful enough to pull the boat against the current. Anglers who wade also have a choice. In some cases, however, it's impractical to proceed upstream because of swift water, deep holes, and impassable banks. But it is almost always better to fish upstream if you can do so without too much difficulty, for several reasons:

- Bass almost invariably face upstream, simply because food drifts with the current. Since they're facing upstream, they're less likely to see an angler approaching from downstream.

- Bass are more likely to see your lure if it's retrieved with the current instead of against it. Assume, for example, that a bass is way-laying beside a stump. If you cast downstream and retrieve upstream, the bass won't see the lure approach. It will come from behind, and might even spook the bass. If you cast upstream, however, the bass will see the lure hit the water and will watch it approach. Besides, a bug or fly looks more natural if it's caught in the current.

- Sounds and vibrations made by wading or bumping things around in a boat carry much farther downstream than they do upstream.

- Anything that bass can taste or smell carries downstream. There is pretty good evidence that a hooked or wounded fish exudes some chemical substance that warns others of its kind of danger, and I believe that this substance can spook bass downstream from you. I've read that merely washing your hands in a stream can have a bad effect on salmon fishing for several miles downstream. I doubt that bass are that sensitive to smells and tastes, but, on the other hand, I think that the angler should have respect for the senses of any fish. One of my nephews is the best creek angler I know, and he won't spit tobacco juice into the water if he's fishing downstream!

Most of the lures discussed in Part Two can be used on a stream, but the mechanics of fishing them are a little different from on an impoundment or a lake. A popping bug won't often sit dead in a stream as it will on a lake; it will drift with the current. You'll have to vary your retrieve to suit the occasion. The current will often be something of a problem, but, on the other hand, you can just as often use the current to your advantage. You can, for example, cast ahead of a likely bass spot, then float your bug into position. Sometimes a lure can be held just out of a treetop or log or some such cover with excellent results, and a bug can be floated under overhanging brush. And merely following the natural drift of the current is sometimes the best possible way to work streamers and bucktails. I might add that some anglers tend to overwork lures in current, and this is especially true of streamers and bucktails; the current itself imparts movement to the lure as a whole as well as to the feathers and hair. So use the current to your advantage instead of fighting it.

A spinner and weighted fly can sometimes be deadly on a stream. My favorite combination is a large weighted Woolly Worm with a size 1 or 2 Colorado spinner and a pork trailer about 1½ times as long as the fly.

So much for streams. I'll end this chapter with an offbeat technique that may infuriate the masters of the dry fly if they ever hear tell of these words. I'm talking about flipping, an old and very effective method of catching bass with an old-fashioned cane pole, long line, and heavy lure. Of course, modern practitioners of the flipping technique will want a rod made especially for that purpose, and the standard flipping rod was developed to appease disgruntled tournament anglers. The complaint was that the cane pole is too long for use on a two-angler tournament boat. The flipping rod that resulted was held to maximum length restrictions—and the standard length isn't necessarily the best length for catching more bass. In some cases, a good pole may work better and a light, long surf-casting rod would surely be a better choice. A heavy fly rod can also be used, and I especially like a 10- or 10½-foot graphite for this purpose.

Of course, the mechanics of flipping are well understood these days and don't require elaboration here. The main advantage of the technique is that the lure is swung out gently under the pole or rod, making a smooth cast that presents the lure accurately and with very little splashdown. The technique depends to a large degree on the use of the left hand (if you hold the rod in your right hand), quite similar to the way an accomplished fly caster hauls line. By pulling a good bit of line out with the left hand, the cast can be made longer and, yes, shooting out some line is also possible. The longer rod also adds to the length of the cast. Most of the bass anglers prefer a heavy weedless jig (⅝ ounce or so) for flipping and use the technique in heavy cover. A lighter lure can be flipped successfully with a fly rod, and it can be quite deadly at times.

One such time came to pass when I needed to catch a mess of bass for guests and also needed to check out a new fly rod. It was supposed to be designed for a

9-weight line, but the thing was too heavy to suit me and it, along with a strong wind, whipped me down before I had enough fish to feed everybody. A little desperate, I ran into a canal that had been cut into the lake island where I lived. As soon as I cut the outboard I saw a boat partly hidden in the grass near a point where the canal split into two legs. I recognized the boat. It belonged to a Florida Cracker who had been fishing the island all his life, and he couldn't abide the fact that it was now private property and had been sectioned off into lots. All of the lots were posted, partly because the inhabitants objected to all the local people coming in with cane poles and cans of worms to catch all the bass that bedded along the banks of the canal. It really was outrageous, and some of these fellows would catch a hundred bedding bass in a single day. (I might add that the locals resented the fact that most of the people who built a house on the lake cleaned out all the grass and lily pads and thick brush along the banks, thereby eliminating the natural habitat for the bass. They had a very good point.) In any case, the trick was to spot a bed with a fish on it, stalk it from the bank, and drop a hook baited with an earthworm on the bottom.

Since I knew the trick, I had already tied a slim 4-inch plastic worm onto my tippet, which was rigged with a size-1 weedless hook without a sinker. Before flipping it out, however, I noticed the hidden boat and headed in that direction with the electric motor on high. I saw the fellow's cane pole sticking up over some bushes. Soon I spotted him hiding behind a palm tree. He had seen me and had hit the ground so that I wouldn't spot him. I eased along, acting as though I didn't know he was there, until I spotted the fish he was after. Easing within casting distance, I stripped off a little line and gently flipped the plastic worm into the far edge of the bed. The bass backed off. The brown worm sank into the white bed, and I let it rest on the bottom, its tail rising just a little. I inched it along and stopped it in the center of the bed. The bass nosed back into the circle of the bed, then rushed forward and sucked up the worm. (I don't think the fish intended to eat the worm, but it wanted the thing out of its bed.) I set the hook and soon had a 3-pounder in the live well.

I reset the weedguard on the worm hook and eased on up the canal until I spotted another bed with another bass of about the same size. I caught it on the first cast and put it into the live well with the other one. This was all I needed, but I knew the Cracker was watching me, so I caught two more before the canal curved around out of his line of sight. Then I went on up to the head of the canal (where I was baiting some turtles) and cleaned the two largest fish, letting the smaller two go. Every now and then I would splash the water a little and talk to an imaginary fish just to make the fellow think I had scored again.

After scaling and gutting the fish, I put the electric motor on high and started out toward the main lake. When I reached the point, the poacher had crawled into the bow of his boat and was pushing off with his foot, getting ready to make a run for it.

"Howdy," I said, nodding. "How's fishing today?"

"I'm not . . . I . . . I . . . I'm just getting started," he said. "How many have you caught?"

"I haven't had a bite," I said, heading for open water.

So . . . sometimes flipping can make the day for you and provide a few fish for the table, even when you're fishing with a fly rod. Don't tell anybody I said that.

CHAPTER 16

HOOKING AND PLAYING BASS

Any angler will miss some strikes and will lose a hooked bass from time to time. But some anglers do connect on a higher percentage of their strikes, and I seem to be one of these. On more than one fishing trip, I have landed more bass than companions who were better casters than I, who seemed to work harder, and who got more strikes. (But also remember that I snatched a bug away from the largest bass I've ever seen.) Although it's true that some anglers are naturally faster than others, anyone can raise his average by giving some thought to the matter. Here are some pointers.

SLACK LINE

I'd guess that more bass are missed because of slack line than for any other single reason. Slack line delays the strike—and anyone who has ever watched a bass suck in and spit out a lure knows that a fraction of a second can be important. Slack line also wastes some (or even all) of the rod's strike arc simply because the angler doesn't get a direct pull on the fish until the slack line is taken up. That isn't entirely accurate, however, because the drag of the line in the water will often set the hook, and the large-diameter fly lines have more drag and surface tension than lines used on spinning or baitcasting gear.

To some extent, slack is inevitable when fishing a stream because the current forms a belly in the line. The same problem—a belly—occurs when casting bugs and other slow lures to a bank ahead of a moving boat. It's impossible to eliminate slack line when fishing a bug properly, but it can be regulated by stripping in or mending the line. The problem is to get the slack out of the line without pulling the bug out of position.

In any case, it pays to be aware of slack line so that you'll be ready to set the hook harder and with a wide strike arc. It will also help to make a long, quick haul with your line hand when you attempt to set the hook with a lot of slack line out.

TIGHT-LINE RETRIEVES

There are several ways to work and retrieve a bug or fly, and too many anglers err by always using the rod tip. It is, of course, sometimes desirable to twitch bugs and flies with the rod tip, or to lift some lures with a long, upward sweep of the rod. Most of the time, however, the bass angler will profit by keeping his rod tip down, pointed directly toward the lure. Holding the rod more or less horizontal and ready has advantages that will be discussed under the next heading.

There are two basic retrieves that permit you to work the lure with little or no rod action, and that can be used to work in slack. The first is to strip in line, making hauls of from a few inches to a few feet. This is a good stop-and-go retrieve, and by pulling smartly on the line you can even make a popping bug do its thing. To make this retrieve, hold the line with the index and middle finger of the rod hand and strip in line with the other hand. By using both hands, you're always in touch with the line and ready to strike at any time.

The second is the hand-twist retrieve, which is good for taking in slack line and for moving the lure with a slow, steady motion. Hold the line between the thumb and forefinger of your left hand (assuming that the rod is in your right hand). Turn your hand and gather in the line with your fingers while maintaining the thumb and forefinger grip. Turn your hand again and grasp more line between your thumb and forefinger. Repeat this procedure for as long as you want to continue with this retrieve. The retrieve is really easier than writing about it.

Whichever way you choose to retrieve, it's very important to keep a firm grip on your fly line. Be ready to respond to a strike at any time. Far too many bass have been missed because the angler dropped the line in order to reach for a pack of cigarettes or to scratch a mosquito bite. Always secure the line under the index and middle fingers of the rod hand before relieving your line hand of its duty. By the way, if bass seem to be psychic in knowing exactly when you drop your line and strike accordingly, it's probably because at such times you let your bug rest longer than usual or let your streamer sink deeper.

WATCH YOUR STRIKE ARC

Too many people have a very bad habit of fishing with their rod sticking straight up. I've even seen the hosts of TV fishing shows do this. The better way is to keep the rod pointed more or less toward the fish during the retrieve. Having a wider strike arc helps in taking in slack and in setting a large hook. The larger the hook, the more important it is to have a good strike arc.

THE BACK-SNAP

Anglers who set the hook with a quick snap or jerk instead of a pull should be aware of what I call the rod's back-snap, a phenomenon that occurs with all rods but is more severe with fiberglass than with bamboo or graphite, and is usually more pronounced in long, limber fly rods. The back-snap can delay the strike for a fraction of a second and cause the tippet to break from impact. Here's an explanation from Charles Waterman's *Modern Fresh and Salt Water Fly Fishing*:

> Before the happy business of subduing the fish, the hook must be set, and the motion is best described as a quick lift of the tip. In other efforts, there may be little difference between a "quick lift" and a "jerk," but there is when a fly rod is involved. The catch is that when a fly rod is jerked quickly and hard, the tip bends toward the fish before it starts moving the other way. This means that instead of taking up slack instantly, the tip actually gives the fish more slack momentarily. Then, as the fisherman's strike is continued, the tip springs back, tightening the line and going with the fisherman's yank, placing a heavy strain on the leader. Not only is it easy to break light tippets this way, but the angler's too sudden strike actually gives a fast fish more time to discard the fly than if the move has been a sharp lift.
>
> The physics of this business is nothing earthshaking. Just hold a rod a few inches above the horizontal to a table, and jerk upward. The tip will flick down and hit the table before following the motion of the rest of the rod. Now, of course, many of us get a little jerk into our lift and the rod may dip a little before coming up, but experienced fishermen learn to keep it to a minimum, and the "quick lift" or "quick sweep" is very different from the jerk.

BE ALERT

The angler who watches his business will usually catch more bass than one who daydreams. Always expect a strike. It helps to keep your eye on a bug or surface lure, and if the bass don't seem to mind, I often choose a bug that I can see, such as fluorescent red or chartreuse. When fishing streamers or other sinking lures, watch your fly line. Any twitch or movement can indicate that a bass has your lure. Think of your fly line as a visual indicator. It is, in fact, a very good one, and is more sensitive than bulky floats.

SHARP HOOKS

In all fishing, it is important that the angler's hook be sharp. This is especially true with large bugs and saltwater flies. Heavy-duty hooks in sizes larger than 3/0 will penetrate better if you take the trouble to triangulate the point with a file, so that it has three cutting edges.

SETTING THE HOOK

It isn't necessary to jerk as hard as some anglers do when they have Texas-rigged a plastic worm, but you must remember to set the hook with some authority. Then quickly lower the rod tip, strip in slack line, and set it again. (This second set is more important with large hooks.)

Just as some anglers connect on a larger percentage of their strikes than their companions, still others actually boat or land more bass after hooking them. Experience will help give you confidence in this matter and will, or should, help you stay cool during the battle. But after landing thousands of bass and not a few lunkers, I hesitate to give anyone advice. Shortly after I was married, my wife and I were fishing with spinning gear one calm afternoon when she tied into a large bass. The thing came out from under an overhanging brush top and hit within 10 feet of the boat. She quickly horsed it within arm's reach and was about, it seemed, to lift it out of the water. Well, that might well have been the thing to do; she might well have got the bass into the boat before it knew what was going on. But I doubted that her 10-pound line would take the strain, and I started yelling at her to give it quarter. The bass hadn't even begun to fight. Anyhow, it got loose pretty quick, and, looking back, I doubt that it was hooked solidly.

She had not yet caught a large bass, and she was upset about the thing. "You should have grabbed it or something," she said, "when I had it at the boat."

Well, I might possibly have netted the fish or "grabbed it," but I still think that I gave her the right advice. This story is complicated by the fact that I caught "her" fish (or an 8-pounder from under the same brush) the next day. I will say only that I advised her in good conscience, and I offer the following considerations in the same spirit:

1. Most fly-rodders, including myself, work a fish in by stripping line. The procedure is similar to a regular stripping retrieve. Some experts, however, advise the angler to bring in fish with the fly reel. One reason is that you'll need to use the reel if you ever go after big game, such as tarpon. To be sure, you can land bass by stripping in line, but you may be developing a bad habit you'll later regret. I might add that I don't regret it. I enjoy working a fish with the line hand, and giving line in the same manner.

2. As everyone knows, the best way to whip a fish is to hold the rod at a high angle, so that the rod will do its thing. I believe that 45 degrees is about right, but you can increase or decrease the effective drag merely by raising or lowering the rod. The higher the rod, the greater the drag caused by friction as the line goes over the rod guides and tip.

3. Holding the rod high, or low, can help you get a bass out of thick cover. In grass, for example, you can sometimes keep a bass from digging in by standing up and holding the rod high over your head. The same high position will help you get a fish over a submerged log if the fish is behind the log (on the far side). If the fish has gone under the log from the near side, however, you'll be trying to bring it under instead of over the log, in which case you should hold the rod as low as possible. You can even stick it down into the water.

4. One problem is what to do when a hooked fish runs toward you. It is, of course, more likely to get off if it has slack line. The only thing I know is to take in the slack as quickly as possible. I normally do this by stripping in line, but you can use the reel if you don't have coils of surplus line lying around. An automatic reel is very good in this situation, but it has limitations and disadvantages that in my opinion outweigh this advantage.

5. Often a large bass will run under the boat, where it may foul the line on the motor. The best bet is to stick the rod down into the water and either try to bring the bass back to your side of the boat or else try to work the rod around either end of the boat. I usually prefer the latter if I have a big fish on and it has gone all the way to the other side of the boat. If at all possible, however, it's better to avoid this situation in the first place. It helps to use the electric motor to swing the bow of the boat one way or the other; just don't cut your line with the electric's prop. Personally, I tilt the kicker out of the water before I start fishing, unless I have good reason to leave it down.

6. Anchor lines in the water have caused many bass anglers to lose some real lunkers. If two anglers are aboard a boat, one can get the anchor up as soon as his companion ties into a trophy bass. If you're fishing alone, drop only the stern anchor and keep the bow-mounted electric in the water; then try to maneuver the boat so that you avoid the anchor line. I also like the new push-button electric anchors. I might add that there is seldom any need to anchor if you're fishing in shallow water and have a good bow-mounted electric motor on your boat. In fact, it's usually best to keep moving unless you have good reason to stop at a certain spot.

7. If you tie into a lunker bass and have enough open water to let it run, take a quick glance at the surplus line that may be coiled at your feet. If it's wrapped around the electric's foot pedal or something, try to free it before things get hectic. The best bet, however, is to keep your line tidy before you tie into that lunker. It also pays to keep the "memory coils" out of your line as much as possible. Stretching the line from time to time will help, and it also helps to have a reel with a large-diameter spool.

8. There are two schools of thought on what to do when a bass jumps, and both are at least partly correct. Some anglers say to point your rod at the fish, thereby giving slack; if you don't give slack, the bass may break your line, what with all that violent head shaking. Others say to keep the line tight, lower the rod, and try to force the fish back down into the water; if you do give slack, they say, the bass is more likely to shake your lure out of its mouth. In my opinion, no single method works best with all kinds of fishing.

If I'm using a heavy plug or jig with a 20-pound-test line, I'll keep my line tight. The heavy line is likely to stand up, and slack line permits the bass to shake the plug or jig too freely. All that weight slinging around can indeed pull the hook out. But with a fly rod and a bug and, say, an 8-pound tippet, it's probably better to give slack by pointing the rod directly at the bass. A bug or fly is very light compared with baitcasting hardware, and the bass isn't as likely to throw it. And trying to horse the bass down during all that frantic movement could well put too much strain on the tippet. Besides, I like to see a fish jump freely.

9. One of the worst mistakes you can make with a lunker bass or other large fish is to take in too much line toward the end of the battle. Never—I mean never—bring the leader into the rod tip and guides. If the knot gets caught, as it very often will, and the fish makes a last-effort lunge, you'll likely lose it, especially with a light tippet. Once your leader gets caught, there's really nothing you can do, since you can't reach out to the end of the fly rod during the critical moment. Smooth knots and ring guides will help—but this problem is easily avoided in the first place by watching what you're doing.

10. If you have a heavy fish on, it's best to work it in by pumping the rod. The trick is to hold the line tight while raising the rod slowly, then lower the rod slowly while you gain line either with your line hand or with your reel. Repeat the process until you have the fish in. Pumping maintains a more constant pressure and gives you a better feeling for what the fish is doing.

11. As I stated in chapter 4, the best way to land a large bass is to grip it by the lower jaw with the thumb and forefinger of your line hand. A lot of anglers prefer to use a net, for one reason or another. If you're one of these, be sure to get a net that's large enough for lunkers and learn how to use it. Always net a bass headfirst. Swooping at it from the rear is definitely a mistake. The best procedure is to lower the net, at an angle, into the water and then bring the bass over it. During the final moments of the battle, keep the net perfectly still until the bass is over it, then simply lift up the net.

In my opinion, it's best to exhaust a bass before attempting to net it. But some experts and bass pros want to bring the fish in as quickly as possible. The saying is that the time to play with a bass is after you have it in the boat. At times, as in heavy cover, it is indeed better to get the fish in as quickly as possible, before it wraps around something and breaks off. And there may be other valid reasons for bringing a fish on in. One of the bass pros told me that he didn't have time to play a fish down.

Also, there is pretty good evidence that a hooked fish will spook any other bass in the immediate area; consequently, the quicker you get a bass out of the water the better are your chances of catching another one nearby. I think there might well be something in this, but personally, I'm going to play an 8-pound bass pretty well if the water is open. My thinking is that one lunker in the hand is worth two in the water.

If you plan to release your fish and want it to survive, bring it in as quickly as possible. I once caught a 7-pound bass on a very light line, playing it for a long time, and it rolled over and died at the boat. Sometimes such a fish can be revived by holding its tail and working it back and forth in the water. Always release the fish gently into the water. In fact, it's best to lip the fish and remove the hook at water level.

12. Finally, the best advice I can give is this: Be sure that your tippet stays in good shape. Inspect it frequently for abrasion and wind knots, which are more common in fly fishing than in other forms of casting. While working on this book, I lost a 5-pound bass by pure negligence. I was fishing for bluegills with a No. 8 bug when I tied into the bass, and I just wasn't expecting such a large fish on so small a lure. After it broke off, inspection showed that I had a wind knot in my 6-pound tippet, and I probably had another one at the point where the line failed. I could have landed that bass if I had been meticulous enough about my tackle. In fact, I had the previous day landed a 7-pounder with the same test tippet—and this fish had another angler's 5/0 worm hook stuck in the corner of its mouth and trailed about 2 feet of 17- or 20-pound monofilament!

I've done some pretty big talking in this chapter and elsewhere in this book about large bass I've taken, but I don't want to give the impression that a fly rod is the best tool for lunkers. It isn't. Usually, the large fish are taken on or near the bottom whereas the fly rod is ideal for fishing on top. The largest bass that I've caught to date on a fly rod weighed a little over 8 pounds.

It hit a bug that I felt was large enough to interest bass but small enough to hook large bluegills. I was fishing along the edge of a grass bed in Florida's Lake Weir, picking up some bull bluegills and an occasional bass, when I found myself hemmed in by two other bassboats. One angler was fishing in a red boat behind me, maybe figuring that I wasn't hurting the bass population with my fly rod. The other boat, with two anglers aboard, was coming toward me. Something had to give, and I sort of treaded water with the electric motor while waiting to see what the oncoming boat was going to do. I was just off a good pocket in the grass, in which I had had a nice strike. While waiting, I made about a dozen casts into the pocket, working the bug very slowly. Off to the right, I noticed the weeds moving. I made a couple more casts and, suddenly, some tiny minnows in the pocket started breaking water. Next cast, I aimed high so that my bug would settle gently, and the bass grabbed it almost before it got wet. The other boats were pretty close by now, and the anglers of course saw my rod bending.

The bass made a run toward the grass on the right side of the pocket, but fortunately I turned it, putting on as much pressure as I thought my tippet would take. Immediately I hit the start button on the foot-controlled pedal and nosed the boat away from the grass. I had my fish where I wanted it, and we fought it out in open water.

When it jumped, however, I suspected that it was hooked deep, and I was afraid that its "teeth" would abrade my tippet.

"Jeeze, what a bass!" said one of the guys in the boat in front of me.

"That's what it's all about," said the guy behind me in the red bassboat.

"Got a net?" said the third one.

The bass jumped again, closer in now. It had practically swallowed my bug.

"Jeeze, what a bass!"

"That's what it's all about."

"Do you need a net? I'll net it for you."

Well, I knew what it was all about and I wanted the other boats to lay off, and I certainly didn't want anybody swatting at my bass with a landing net under any circumstances and certainly not from another boat. Anyhow, the bass went around the boat a couple of times before it tired out. Cautiously, I brought it on in and gripped its lower jaw. Then I stood up in the boat and showed my fish.

"Jeeze, what a bass!"

"I'd have netted that fish."

"That's what it's all about," said the guy in the red boat.

The next afternoon, shortly before sundown, I thought maybe I ought to try the same grass bank again. When I headed the boat around the point, however, I saw that someone was fishing the pocket. He had anchored his red boat out a ways and was whipping a brand-new fly rod around, seeming to have difficulty in getting the bug out, much less into the pocket. Recognizing me, he redoubled his efforts.

This fellow seemed quite serious about his fishing, so I headed my boat on up the grass bank without telling him that he wasn't doing what it was all about. His quickness to try a fly rod, however, together with the success I had been having with popping bugs and flies, is what got me to thinking about writing this book. I can only hope that it will help a few readers learn for themselves what it's all about.

INDEX